12 95

SO-CTH-314

Action Strategies for Managerial Achievement

Action Strategies
for
Managerial
Achievement

Dalton E. McFarland

A Division of American Management Associations

Library of Congress Cataloging in Publication Data

McFarland, Dalton E
    Action strategies for managerial achievement.

    Includes index.
    1. Management. I. Title.
HD31.M16   658.4   76-51446
ISBN 0-8144-5434-8

First Printing

For

Jean A. McFarland

Preface

This book is for managers in all types of organizations who seek fulfillment, achievement, and advancement through strategies for creative action.

Managers at supervisory and middle levels of organization have become acquainted with modern management techniques through internal and external training programs. What such managers need is a way of integrating and applying this knowledge in order to become more effective persons in their organizations. This book will help readers who work for organizations to interpret and coordinate what they already know. By building personal strategies for successful accomplishment, managers can benefit both themselves and the organizations for which they work.

Creativity in recent years has fallen into disrepute as a management concept. No doubt this is due to the mystique that often surrounds it as well as to the shallowness of the gimmicks by which it is often advanced as a simple answer to complex problems. Shorn of its mystery and fads, however, creativity should be seen as a set of attitudes and actions available to anyone. It can be practiced and learned by anyone. Thinking creatively frees the manager from unnecessary organizational constraints and greatly illuminates the contingencies and problems that confront him or her.

Many persons have helped in the preparation of this book, and I am grateful for their ideas and suggestions. The managers, executives, and administrators I have interviewed or who have been my clients provided invaluable perspectives and examples.

I thank my colleagues at the University of Alabama in Birmingham for their friendship and for provocative discussions of the ideas in this book. Dean M. Gene Newport and Dr. W. Jack Duncan of the School of Business made valuable suggestions and provided encouragement and support. Miss Marcia Stokes worked faithfully to put the manuscript in final form. Finally, my wife, to whom this book is dedicated, contributed valuable ideas and excellent critiques of the work as it progressed. To all these people I am in great debt, though any faults remaining must be ascribed to me alone.

Dalton E. McFarland

Contents

CHAPTER
1
Creative Managerial Action

More than ever, today's organizations need managers who possess the skills of management and administration and who know how to develop these skills in others. A manager is, in fact, a merchant of managerial skills and abilities and a professional in the application of management knowledge within an organization.

This book tells how to develop and use the skills of management in an organization. Its central theme is creative managerial action—the transformation of managerial knowledge into effective, economical results through bold, imaginative, and analytical strategies. Creative managerial action emphasizes the force and vigor with which you can revitalize your work. It dramatizes your powers of initiative, intelligence, and influence in an organization. It implies that fulfillment and a sense of achievement can be yours through the work you are paid to do. It is reflected in your zest for life and your enthusiasm for work.

The manager today is a vitally important person in our society. The complex organizations and institutions which serve our needs require highly developed managerial capabilities. Accordingly, organizations of all types must constantly attract, develop, and utilize managerial talent. But persons who have a demonstrated or a potential capacity for successful organizational action and decision are always in short supply. Therefore, search and development processes should continuously be at work.

1

Organizations require a large share of society's managerial talent, and they produce a large part of the supply. Managerial knowledge and skills spring from two main sources: formal training and acquired experience. These two sources mutually reinforce one another, and managers need the benefits of both. From one individual to another, the emphasis on either source may vary, but the use of formal training to give additional meaning to experience is widespread.

The ability to manage effectively is not naturally or automatically present in individuals, although personality, temperament, and physical attributes may greatly influence managerial performance. The need for training in addition to experience reflects the knowledge explosion in society generally, as well as the trend toward professionalization and specialization of the individual's role in organizations and in society. Self-development efforts can do much for the energetic, ambitious individual, but formal education and training provide larger increments of knowledge in a shorter time. Furthermore, formal training yields perspectives that can make one's day-to-day experiences more relevant and meaningful.

Today's manager needs both training and guided experience not only for better job performance but also for advancement to greater responsibilities. Successful managers are highly mobile. They are upwardly oriented and conscious of the possibilities for enlarging the scope of their experiences. In the advancement of their careers, managers encounter critical turning points at which the need for changing from one organization to another becomes apparent. Such moves usually entail an improvement in pay, status, and responsibilities. Professional attitudes and aspirations help to develop one's career based on accomplishment and fulfillment of potential.

The Organization Base

Your organization is the setting for your managerial career. It is your base of operations, providing the incentives, the purposes, the resources, and the opportunities for your development as a manager. In turn, you are charged with serving it well and fulfilling your commitments to it. To do this, you must not only know your job but also your organization in every detail. And since everything is subject to change, you must continuously make your studies and observations.

Yet you need not, and in many cases should not, marry the organization for life. For its fullest development, your career may require that you work in a well-selected series of organizations. Just as an organization makes its periodic evaluations of you and your work, so too should you make your own personal evaluations of it. One of the main criteria to use in such an evaluation is the organization's capacity to help you develop your ability to handle managerial responsibilities.

To build backlogs of reserve manpower for coping with growth and change, organizations have development programs and policies. Judicious use of these resources can pave the way for the critical turning points that will inevitably arise in your career. It is up to you as well as the organization to make these work for the mutual interests of both.

The Human Factor

If rational behavior were the sole determinant of a goal, you would be able to proceed logically and trust the outcome to performance. Unfortunately, you face greater complexity than the purely rational approach suggests, for an organization is not only a duty station where work is done; it is also a great arena for competition among aspirants for power and influence. Competition introduces nonrational, subjective factors into promotion, pay, and other decisions. And just by being human, people, including yourself, are rendered incapable of acting with complete rationality and objectivity at all times.

Your career evolves not only out of what you know and what you can do but also out of power struggles, opportunism, political *savoir-faire*, chance, personalities, and the operating styles and philosophies of your fellow managers. Skills in these areas are precisely those that cannot be directly taught in formal education and training programs, and they are the principal reason for weighting the experience factors so heavily in managerial effort. This does not mean that formal training and education should be avoided, however. Both formal training and experience are needed because they are mutually reinforcing.

This book examines the best of current thinking as it applies to your career planning and development as an effective and successful manager. The emphasis will be on creative managerial action, illuminated by the lessons of both experience and research. The object is to assist you in improving your own performance through better understanding of how the creative manager thinks and acts. There is no simple set of rules or guidelines to take the place of careful, strategic thought and planning.

The Creative Manager

What makes a manager creative? Can any manager become more creative? Can a manager be *too* creative? You need answers to these questions before reading further in this book.

We begin by recognizing that some people are more creative than others. Not everyone is noticeably creative, but most people are creative in at least some aspects of their lives or some of the time. The reason is that circumstances as well as personal characteristics have a lot to do with how creative a person is. Workers on an assembly line have little scope in which to be creative in their formal work, no matter how creative they may be as individuals. Studies have shown that these workers tend to express their creativity in their informal associations with each other.

Creativity is a matter of degree. It is not a question of having it. A person is not equally creative in all aspects of his life. An artist may be highly creative in oils or water colors but not in getting meals or in sustaining a healthy marriage. You may be creative in your home workshop but not at the office. A writer may create fascinating fiction but show very little imagination when it comes to choosing clothes.

Although creativity itself is one of life's great mysteries, psychologists have nevertheless found out a lot about creative people. These individuals have a fresh way of seeing and making sense of what they see and experience. Part of creativity is heightened perception, the ability to recognize significant aspects of the world that others miss. It is also the ability to make connections, to relate things that at first seem unrelated. A third characteristic of a creative person is the courage and drive to make use of the perceived interactions and to apply them to achieve some new result. Also, a certain playfulness of mind is necessary. "To stimulate creativity," Einstein said, "one must develop the childlike inclination for play and the childlike desire for recognition."

Daydreaming may also be a factor in problem-solving creativity. In a study of daydreaming males, one researcher found that the most frequent activity was trying to get at useful clues to solve a problem, especially among persons aged 24 through 34, a group that sustains heavy demands from family and job. According to this study, daydreaming happens to almost everyone without conscious initiation, and in all age groups except the oldest, daydreams occur when people aren't paying attention to an immediate task.* You can get constructive payoffs from the kind of daydreaming that gives the powers of your mind freedom to speculate, innovate, and synthesize.

Thinking Vertically and Laterally

Creativity is largely a thought process, the ability to generate ideas and ways of carrying them out. Ideas are the lifeblood of an organization, essential for its nurture and growth. They are the raw material of the thought processes which lead to creative results.

Organizations need people who can think. Thus it is not only those whom we call leaders who require vision, imagination, and resourcefulness. Thinking, however, is hard work because it thrives best when the thinker can at least temporarily detach himself from the constraints of his present situation. Such detachment requires what is known as sequential thinking.

Sequential thought links ideas for analytical or creative purposes. This entails recognizing the consequences of one thought or idea for other thoughts or ideas. It makes for deeper, more significant thought and is a necessary antidote to random thinking in which notions flit through the mind one at a time without having much consequence.

*Leonard M. Giambra, "Daydreaming Across the Life Span: Late Adolescent to Senior Citizen," *International Journal of Aging and Human Development*, Spring 1974, pp. 114–120.

Sequential thought may be vertical or lateral. Vertical thought is in the traditional, problem-solving mode. It consists of perceiving natural patterns and focal events in the current situation, then developing ideas, concepts, approaches, or points of view. Once the thought patterns are organized, methods of logic and mathematics can be used to generate and evaluate solutions. The process is vertical because each new layer of thought goes on top of what is already there. The base remains, with progress measured in terms of results at each series of steps. Factors irrelevant to the base are rejected.

But what if the base itself is not adequate? Then we should begin to think laterally, that is, restructure the situation from a different base. Concepts are changed, not merely developed vertically. Lateral thinking generates new ideas and does not narrowly define what is relevant. It liberates the mind from habit and from repetitive, conventional thought. Thus it organizes information differently than logic would dictate to force the emergence of new patterns and to generate alternative configurations. Thought is sideways rather than straight ahead.

Vertical and lateral thinking go hand in hand and are both highly desirable in organizations. Most of us are trained to think vertically, but the creative person goes beyond this to attain broader perspectives and new concepts of the present as well as the future. The aim of both types of thinking is effectiveness.

Reliance on vertical thinking is fostered by the tendency of most managers to be satisfied with the present situation. Why be creative if there is no need to? Why not wait until a problem forces creativity? When a problem arises, solve it. People who have technical, highly specialized training often lack creativity because professional and technical training teaches them to think vertically. They become disoriented when the convenient platforms on which their efforts rest are swept away by changing circumstance.

Vertical thinking is illustrated by the case in which a company's vice-president of development resigned. Everyone speculated about who the president would choose to fill the vacancy. But all were startled when the president, using lateral thinking, changed the basic premises of the entire organization by abolishing the position instead of filling it.

Receptivity to Creative Ideas

You are creative if you have some of the characteristics of the creative person and choose to apply the creative part of your nature to your managerial responsibilities. You have to be persistent in not invoking the thousands of excuses that stand in the way of creative effort. "My boss won't let me do it" or "nobody around cares" are the favorite rationalizations of many who don't try for creative approaches.

Creativity is something of a mystical happening—an intense yet relaxed involvement of the psyche with concrete experience. Creative managers make use of their subconscious. They may let the details of a problem rest in the back of their minds, during which time the patterns of thought rearrange themselves, grow, fade, reassert themselves, and finally bring out new insights and new patterns. Keeping open to the ideas of others and listening are powerful devices of the creative mind at work.

Every manager can work more creatively. As a consultant, I have suggested creative strategies to hundreds of managers, many of whom settle back to comfortable routines and ordinary answers. Sometimes managers misjudge the expectations of others. Often they are right in believing that "my organization just isn't ready for this one yet." There is a time to be creative, and often that time is when the problem is toughest, people are the most discouraging, and there are the least grounds for hope. Stress and tension cry out for creative approaches.

Do discouraging, unfavorable circumstances quash the creative urge or spur it into action? This is where one's personal characteristics enter: courage, intelligence, energy, imagination, and resourcefulness help the individual persist and to accept challenges. On the other hand, a timid, dependent, insecure, or lazy manager may turn aside creative ideas.

If you are in an organization that consistently turns off creative urges in you, you will acquire habits that produce ordinary, lusterless performance by accepting defeat as inevitable. What you need then is a creative strategy either for leaving the organization or for helping it to change its ways. You have a strong inner need for an organization that brings out the best in you: your creative side.

A manager can be *too* creative in a number of ways. If you are the only creative person in your group, you will be a loner, a misfit, with all the discomforts this entails. Some types of creativity are dysfunctional to the organization and to the individual, such as creativity directed toward selfish or dishonest aims. The creative scoundrel, thief, agitator, or crisis provoker helps no one and may do more harm than good. Creativity in the expression of animosity or hostility is self-defeating. Creativity coupled with venality, vindictiveness, or prevarication is bad for everyone.

Creativity in the generation of useful ideas and innovations is generally the best direction in which to move. However, your creative brainchildren will be examined and evaluated by others, some of whom are capable of objective judgment, but some of whom are not. An idea can be rejected because it is too good or because it is too bad. The idea that is too good finds resistance and delay among those who are made to seem incompetent by it or among those who feel they should have thought of the idea themselves. Your creative idea can also be rejected for a host of nonrational reasons.

The validity of your ideas and creative strategies is subject to testing by those in authority and by those who may be affected by them. Thus, you will need to be ready to meet these tests by marshaling evidence and other pertinent information and by devising methods of persuasion appropriate to the situation.

You might feel that a worthy idea should stand on its own merit. But this is seldom the case, especially when what you are pushing involves change. The merits have to be first demonstrated and then accepted. The evaluations of others are not entirely based on logic: there will often be emotional and even irrational elements. This applies whether your change is directed upward, downward, or laterally in the organization—to your boss, your subordinates, or to your peers.

Creative managers know how to handle rejection of their ideas constructively. Essentially this means carefully considering the basis for adverse judgments. Criticisms are used to refine ideas and reshape them for an opportune rebirth. The creative frame of mind is open to suggestion and analysis and receptive to inputs from others. Contrary to popular notions, the creative mind does not operate in isolation. It interacts with other minds and comes up with a new synthesis or new formulation. But you have to learn to accept disappointment and frustration at times. It takes courage to accept no for an answer or to bide one's time.

Analysis may show that substantive criticisms surrounding the introduction of a new idea do not warrant discarding it but that one's timing is off. The creative idea or act is creative precisely because it is a bit ahead of its time. However, it cannot be too far removed from the sense of the situation to which it will be applied. A manager who would be a leader needs to recognize when the time for creative action has come. Timing is vitally important.

Creative Influence

Executives vary widely in their ability to make their influence felt, whether with boss, subordinates, or colleagues. Much depends on their physical and mental energy and on their drives, habits, and temperament. But by viewing the climb to the top in a business organization as a process of extending one's sphere of creative influence in all three directions—up, down, and sideways—executives can acquire fresh perspectives for accomplishing results. They will be better prepared to develop their administrative skills. Planning, organizing, controlling, directing, and deciding will have more meaning when tied in with an understanding of their working relationships with others.

At this point numerous difficulties arise. Inhibiting conditions emerge from the interaction factors in human relationships. When one seeks to effect a change in a situation that concerns only physical properties, such as an inventory or a machine, given actions produce generally predictable and measurable results. When, however, one wishes to influence or change the behavior of a person, that person acts or reacts uniquely and his reactions are predictable only in a very general sense. Thus, if you slap a person's face, you can usually (but not always) expect anger. But if you ask someone for support on your pet project, you cannot be sure how that person will cast his vote.

A further difficulty is found in what happens to power, authority, and responsibility. As you gain increasingly effective influence in an organization, you will eventually acquire increased authority and power. Power and authority relationships become more complex, more sensitive, more risky, and more laden with tension and strain as they increase. A familiar example will make this clear. Suppose a committee member comes up with what appears to be the best solution for a problem on which the committee is working. The committee chairman says, "Joe, this was your idea and it is a good one. We are going to count on you to carry out this plan. Since it was your idea, we feel that you are the best one to get the job done." This leaves Joe with a dilemma: if he rejects the suggestion, he indicates a lack of confidence in his idea and in his own ability to pursue it. If he accepts the responsibility, he has a tough new piece of work on his hands.

It is, however, the administrative, organizational hierarchy and its associated management modes that both nourish and constrain the creative forces of the advancing executive. Nourishing forces are inherent in the problems and challenges the organization can provide, along with resources that make it possible to do interesting things. The constraining forces come from the greater remoteness from operating activities, the increased length of communication channels, and above all, the larger scope of authority and responsibility.

Two basic coping patterns can be discerned in the way executives respond to the challenges and constraints. One pattern is the bold, assertive, aggressive behavior of the creative manager, which can best be denoted as the "active" pattern. The other pattern is the weak, timorous, unassertive behavior of the manager labeled "passive." These patterns represent polar types.

Although one seldom encounters a manager who perfectly fits one polar type or the other, studying both extremes in detail throws light on the more typical intermediate patterns of behavior. Some of the primary characteristics of each polar type are listed here:

The Active Manager	*The Passive Manager*
Creative	Unimaginative
Intrepid	Unassertive
Resolute	Vacillating
Audacious	Docile

The Active Manager	*The Passive Manager*
Daring	Malleable
Adventurous	Defeatist
Strong	Conformist
Secure	Weak
Courageous	Acquiescent
Confident	Subservient
Enthusiastic	Deferential
Independent	Insecure
Forward-Looking	Submissive
Bold	Timid

The active manager is action-oriented, even when the going gets tough. The passive manager is delay-oriented, even when the going is easy. Passivity often results from forms of insecurity, as illustrated by the words of a successful president of a manufacturing corporation, who said, "I did not dare tell any of my top executives or any of the shop workers that I was about to complete a merger with another firm." Such timidity is an inner flaw in the form of a pervasive escapism. "Passive man" represents a new character type to put alongside Riesman's "other-directed man" and Whyte's "organization man." The contrasting behavior patterns of active and passive managers are these:

The Active Manager	*The Passive Manager*
Makes timely decisions	Tends to avoid decisions
Sizes up the job and does it	Procrastinates
Seeks contacts with others, is gregarious	Avoids people, especially those who cause difficulties
Delegates	Withholds authority as a self-protective device
Faces situations realistically	Is overly cautious
Welcomes new ideas and methods	Avoids change
Communicates willingly	Fails to communicate
Has a democratic demeanor	Has an autocratic demeanor
Confronts problems, situations	Hides problems or hides from problems

The Active Manager	*The Passive Manager*
Monitors situations and follows up	Fails to monitor or follow up
Admits mistakes	Blames others, makes up excuses
Is constantly learning	Is unwilling to learn

A given manager does not exhibit the same degree of activeness or passiveness at all times or in all situations. One may habitually gravitate toward being either active or passive, but the direction in which one leans is largely affected by one's own efforts. Therefore, in making adjustments in one's career, it is possible over time to shift in one direction or the other. Furthermore, some organizational situations may call for a measure of passivity rather than the aggressive attacks of the adventurous, while others cry out for bold action. Wisdom is needed to sense the requirements of each situation.

But courage rather than timidity is the hallmark of creative managers. Put to the test of staking millions of company dollars on decisions having clear elements of risk, we see executives making truly courageous decisions.

On the other hand, we have declarations by men like Ordway Tead, Marshall Dimock, and Clarence Randall, all of whom have talked in one way or another about "the lonely art of decision making." With all the help of teams and committees, the decision maker at the apex of a situation finally retires to his office in solitude, knowing that he will have no one to blame but himself if things go wrong.

Courage is required in the little things that make up the administrator's day as well as the big events. The momentous decisions that change the course of an organization do not happen every day. When they do happen, the administrator has the counsel and support of his fellows. It is in the many day-to-day events of his association with colleagues and subordinates that the timid acts of the passive administrator are most likely to occur, unnoticed by many—even the administrator himself. He slides into a comfortable habit which has the cumulative effect of limiting his performance.

Here are some examples of the courageous manager in action:

He has the fortitude to say "no" to requests that are not ethically right.

He says "no" to the good guys who are popular.

He admits having limitations by asking the advice of others.

He says "I don't know" rather than having an answer for everything.

He is willing to disagree with a superior if his judgment deems it appropriate.

The distinctive attribute of the passive manager is the need for self-defense. Why did the president-owner of a manufacturing corporation mentioned previously negotiate a merger without telling his staff? While no one can fully know his inner motivation, he went on to say that "it would get everyone upset" and "what I really did was protect my people from unnecessary worry in case the merger fell through." Such concern for others is frequently a mask covering the fears and anxieties of the decision maker.

The passive administrator abhors standing between organization tasks and goals on the one hand and the needs and demands of his own staff on the other. Avoidance of these pressures is couched in terms thought readily acceptable to others, but in actuality his explanations are likely to be a rationalization for an unwillingness to act.

Organizational structure and design characteristics greatly affect active-passive behavior. For example, in the flat organization structure, the communication chains are short, the authority hierarchies are less rigid, and the tone and morale are more supportive. Such an organization cannot harbor many passive managers, for all are highly visible and operate under conditions of heavy personal responsibility and accountability.

In tall, highly bureaucratic organizations, many devices offer protection to the passive or timid manager. For example, by aligning oneself with the appropriate in-group power structure, and by acting in such a way as to support or at least not to antagonize this power group, one's position will be secure no matter how one acts. The creative manager on the inside of the power group currently in control of the corporate organization structure can even afford to be a nonentity as an administrator. If one is properly aligned and upwardly oriented, one does not need to be particularly concerned about subordinates or people on the outside of the in-group power structure or even about task performance.

Another key characteristic of passive administrators is the avoidance of dissent. It is a problem for them to handle their own dissenting feelings as well as those of subordinates. Active managers incorporate dissent into their work patterns as a necessary part of the organizational life, though they may attempt to handle it carefully and in perspective. Timid managers, on the other hand, ignore, ridicule, or label dissenters as agitators or troublemakers.

Active creative managers possess the skill of communicating dissent when it is important under the guidelines of their consciences. They register dissent knowing the risks and that only in part can they minimize these risks. Not being afraid to dissent from those above them, they are in a better position to understand and successfully handle the dissent of their own subordinates.

In summary, to be influential, the creative manager learns to size up the key elements of each situation. Most situations provide opportunities for action and decision that require keen judgment and risk taking. The creative manager also has to assess the relative importance of the key elements and the probable effects of alternative moves. Most executives can increase the breadth and depth of their influence by practicing the skills of size-up and analysis before taking action. Although most executives are more influential than they realize, the problem is to direct, control, and channel their influence toward effective ends. The creative manager rejects passive patterns of behavior wherever possible and seeks to follow courageous, forward-moving paths that earn the respect of others even when they disagree.

CHAPTER
2

Action-Centered Goals

All human beings, by virtue of their humanity, have goals. To be alive is to pursue goals. The organization for which you work also has goals. The foundation of an organization's existence is the application of scarce resources to the attainment of goals.

One key task of the creative manager is to choose goals for himself. Another is to choose or influence the goals of his organization. The two processes of choice are interrelated, each one influencing the other. They have much in common, yet to the individual they may appear widely divergent.

Goals are constantly changing, so the creative manager periodically reviews and revises his goals. Progress toward goals necessitates their reappraisal for relevance, appropriateness, and practicality. The alternative, not a sound one, is to drift aimlessly from day to day, doing only what is required to get through to quitting time.

Few goals are actually achieved, at least in their entirety. Total or final achievement would result in complacency for the individual or the end of the organization's *raison d'être*. A goal, by definition, is something that you intend to achieve. Therefore to select goals is to determine the guidelines by which you or the organization can judge particular actions.

Congruence of Goals

Organizations are more effective and the members of an organization are more satisfied when there is a reasonable degree of congruence between personal and organizational goals. Congruence of goals means that the individual's goals and the organization's goals are served simultaneously. That is, the same managerial actions tend to serve the purposes of both. The relationship between you and your organization is dynamic, which means that it has a life and character of its own. Despite the forces of change, both you and the organization you work for must perceive and receive benefits of mutual value if the relationship is to endure.

To achieve congruence of goals, both the organization and the individual must know them. Such knowledge may take many forms—policy manuals, annual corporate reports, bulletins, pamphlets, records, or planning memorandums. Setting forth goals in these forms makes possible the detection of incongruencies and the need for clarification and change.

Over time, incongruencies may become manifest. In the give and take that pervades your service to an organization, there will be times when you feel that it is demanding too much from you. The workload may suddenly increase; associates or superiors may seem intolerable; stresses, strains, and pressures may seem overwhelming. You may feel compelled to accept tasks, duties, or responsibilities that are at odds with your basic plans or preferences. Carefully mapping your own goals will help you prevent the organization from deflecting you from your central course and protect you from casual, unplanned, or expedient bending to circumstantial pressure.

Sometimes you feel that everything is going your way, and that you cannot possibly deserve all the benefits the organization is eager to bestow. Most of the time, however, managers find their feelings fluctuating somewhere between elation and despondency. Moods encroach on our patterns of rational thought. The creative manager recognizes these moods, and tries to avoid captivity by the extremes of pessimism and optimism. Goal planning provides the perspectives you can use to avoid euphoria and complacency, minimize anxiety and uncertainty, and maintain a sense of direction.

Complexity of Goals

One difficulty in achieving goal congruency is that both people and organizations have multiple, complex goals. The creative manager selects personal goals while giving careful thought to those of the organization. The effective organization selects its goals with sensitivity to the needs of its members. Nevertheless, the opportunities for difficult problems to arise are inherent in the nature of goals systems.

Within an organization, all individuals share some goals in common, but there are also differences in their goals. No two people have the same set of goals, though particular goals may be identical or similar. Thus creative managers know that not everyone is seeking what they are seeking, and few are using the same range of strategies to pursue those goals. Some managers are unaware of the goals of others, and individuals have different perceptions of their own and others' goals.

It is helpful to think of goals in terms of their pattern—the way they form a cohesive, intelligible whole. This is known as the goal matrix, or goal structure. In the matrix, goals exist at a number of levels and across the divisional or departmental structure. Understanding the goal matrix is necessary for effective goal planning because it depicts goals in relation to each other.

Actually there are two goal matrixes, one for the manager and one for his organization. Each has two dimensions—the horizontal and the vertical. The two matrixes overlap, and the extent of this overlap is a measure of their congruency.

The horizontal dimension distributes organizational goals (and other elements) among specialized units, such as departments, divisions, sections, or branches. The vertical dimension distributes goals and subgoals by level of organization. Thus the pattern of goals is fitted to the prevailing pattern of organization structure.

The matrix for individual goals is less clear but no less significant. Horizontally the manager has goals that pertain to his formal and informal relationships to other managers and organizational units. For example, he may desire to acquire knowledge and experience through transfer to different specialties. Vertically the manager has some goals that are directed upward toward people or units higher up and others that are directed downward toward subordinates or lower units in the hierarchy. Personal goals are fitted not only to this structural base but also along a time and priority dimension.

One important element of complexity with respect to goals is that of determining real or legitimate goals. Within the goal repertoire of a manager, for example, a mixture of goals is affirmed and desired that will bring agreement and recognition by others. The manager may also have goals which lie hidden beneath the surface, for they are not acceptable personally or by colleagues or by society in general. Consequently, to the extent that one's true goals are less than fully acceptable in a public way, goals will be covered, hidden, and not made explicit. Likewise, there may be "pseudo goals"—ones that operate like real goals but are understood to be only for show or talk, not for real action. The reason for this sham is that the attainment of the pseudo goal would wipe out all the conditions which made it seem desirable in the first place. For example, if Marxism were to succeed in destroying capitalism, the economic problems faced by capitalism would remain, but it would then be up to Marxism to prevent its faults and difficulties.

The manager who is highly ambitious for advancement and power may find that such goals collide with the goals of others. Since this situation, if flagrant, could lead to interpersonal conflict with those who appear to stand in the way, these goals are either held dormant in the manager's mind, or they are presented in more acceptable terms. Therefore, expressed goals are not always one's ultimate goals, since they are subject to transference that renders them publicly acceptable. Situations vary in the degree to which actual goals are subjected to this process of transference by the existence of organizational constraints.

For the creative manager, the conflict-transference problem argues for great care in making goals known to others. Announced goals should be realistic. The new office clerk who announces that "some day I am going to be president of this company" may be admired for having an adventuresome and daring attitude but criticized for unnecessarily overstating a goal.

Goal planning for the creative manager entails considering all of the dimensions of the two matrixes. In addition, it requires decisions as to timing and relevance A critical aspect of this planning centers in the strategies for adopting, announcing, and pursuing goals that are not only appropriate but realistic.

Where Do Goals Come From?

It will help to consider how organizational goals originate. You may think at first that organizational goals come from leaders, bosses, or administrators. It is true that someone in authority chooses goals from which instructions or orders for action are derived. They authenticate the organization's goal structure. This process is observable in every organization, but we must look beyond it to get a clearer understanding of goals. We must ask where leaders or administrators find the goals they choose.

Note first that organizational goals are selected from a large number of possible alternatives. The manager who announces a goal has presumably considered these alternatives, weighed their advantages and disadvantages, and made it possible for the members of the group to focus on reasonable choices. This results in concentration of effort, attention, and resources on a manageable range of activities.

To consider alternative goal possibilities, the manager has to study many complex factors within and without the organization. Some of the most important goal formation results from needs and pressures in the organization's environment. Therefore it is important for the manager to examine the significant elements in the environment, to know what is going on in the community, the economy, other organizations, government, and the world at large. The manager tries to observe enough of what is happening to judge the relative priorities of the information gathered and the relevance of what is observed. Clearly managers must make many intuitive judgments, forecasts, evaluations, and appraisals based on as much hard data as time, energy, and money permit.

The outside origins of goals are all too often not noticed by the managers inside. It is easy to conceive of the organization as containing its own dominant power centers, domains of independent, autonomous power that initiate everything that happens. If this were the case and all centers of organizational action were independent of outside forces, there would be no constraining limits on action, no boundaries or disciplines that stabilize and give meaning to what the organization does. For example, a company must be sensitive to its market opportunities. To be sure, it might try to shape its market opportunities through product design or advertising, but in the end it must meet the tests of the marketplace. No other objectives can take the place of these. Another example is that of a government bureau created to carry out the mandates of a legislature. The law prescribes the purposes and activities of the bureau, and its administrators, while they have many flexibilities as to policies and procedures, are ultimately subject to the requirements of the legislature's intent.

Goals come from within the organization as well as from with-out. Managers who think creatively about their jobs see that change is constant, and improvement is persistently demanded. After external goal formation processes have brought analyzed aims and purposes into the organization, those inside must do the fine tuning—make applications and interpretations and break the larger objectives into manageable delegations for the various units of the organization. This indicates that there exists in every organization a range or hierarchy of objectives. At each level, then, every manager has a responsibility for setting objectives and determining the scope of appropriate activities for his unit. In so doing he is part of a larger system of effort but nonetheless a critical part.

It is important also to note that objectives for the organization, especially the broad overall objectives originating in environmental forces, are typically selected by groups rather than by individual leaders. To be sure, the decisions may be announced and authenticated by a top leader or chief executive. But they are more typically the product of a team decision and the work of large staffs of researchers and specialists whose task is to monitor the environment, test ideas, make plans, and forecast the future. The problems of modern organizations are so complex that most if not all major decisions could not be made by an individual but must be the product of group effort.

Now a word about your personal goals. Most managers would agree that they work for a living, to meet the economic needs of everyday life. But most acknowledge also that there is more to working than the money. Personal goals such as the desire for recognition, esteem, and the advancement of one's career are important. An important nonfinancial goal for many managers is achievement.

Your personal image is in part made up of the goals you select for yourself. The goals you seek tell others a lot about you. This is why recruiting officers often ask about your goals. If you *are* in the game for money, it is probably wise to acknowledge this at the outset, for it will quickly become apparent in your actions. Money is not in and of itself a bad goal, but it can be if it is pursued to the exclusion of all others. There are times when money is very important, such as when you are underpaid and you seek to get what you are worth. There is a time to be aggressive about money in your relationship with your employer. However, money pursued without achievement or results or as an end in itself is in most cases a sterile endeavor.

Pay is important because it can be the common denominator for the evaluation of individuals in a competitive environment. Thus it translates into self-esteem. You need the raise you demand not only because you have more places to spend it but also because it is a measured reflection of your worth and value to the organization that others, both inside and outside the organization, will understand.

There are other reflections of your image, best considered in the form of questions you have to ask yourself in your career planning. What kinds of recognition are important to you other than money? In what kind of an organization can you appear at your best? In what group can you develop most easily a sense of belonging? What kind of people do you like to be associated with, to spend time with? What tasks and skills can you best perform? How much ambiguity can you tolerate, and how certain do you want the future to be? It is in your answers to these questions and others like them that your goals are set and your image is defined for others.

Expectations and Aspirations

It is a fact of organizational life that both your personal goals and organizational goals will change. Sometimes goals will be changed for you or for the organization by circumstance—factors over which you have little or no control or influence. These kinds of changes have to be adapted to after careful thought about their evident and potential effects on you and your work.

Other kinds of goals are within your scope of influence, and depend heavily on choices you yourself make. These goals, too, require careful thought and planning. Consciously planned goals need to be realistic—that is, within your range of probability for achieving them. Yet the goals must be high if your highest goal is excellence. Most managers do not achieve as much as they could because they do not have sufficiently high expectations of themselves, and no one has succeeded in raising their sights. George Odiorne expressed these ideas well:

> . . . excellence in management consists of setting great goals—
> and in achieving them. The two parts of the process are essential
> in measuring excellence. Without goals and objectives chosen in
> advance, the final results may not be measured, since their
> achievement may be due to windfall (or good luck) alone. Great
> goals without matching achievement may be the sign of an idle
> dreamer. *

The creative manager gives conscious thought to his personal goals, setting them high enough to provide a significant challenge to his abilities, yet not so high as to be impossible or impracticable to attain.

Ethical Goals

Your own set of ethical values, judgments, and beliefs is put to the test in any organization you work for. Your first affiliation with the organization presumes some degree of congruence between your values and those of the organization, insofar as these could be analyzed prior to employment. At least you did not encounter any signals that prevented your acceptance of a position for reasons of ethics. As your relationship with the organization matures, you will have many opportunities to verify your

---

*"A Search for Objectives in Business—The Great Image Hunt," *Michigan Business Review*, January 1966, p. 24.

original impressions or to take note of changes in your first perceptions.

As a manager you will see others not only holding values different from your own but acting in accordance with them. The fact that their beliefs differ from yours does not necessarily make theirs wrong and yours right. Generally accepted standards of conduct protect individuals, organizations, and society from harm, instability, and loss.

Acts of theft, embezzlement, or other forms of lawbreaking are clearly wrong and may be punished according to law. But the whole domain of human activity in an organization is clothed with a more complex ethical obligation than obeying the letter of the law. To steal corporate funds is a serious crime, but to accuse one's competitor-subordinate of false charges is questionable ethically even though it violates no law.

Both personal and organizational goals have this important element of ethics. You will face many situations in which you and your conscience will have to decide whether standards of proper conduct have been transgressed. You can test your goals and those of the organization by asking such questions as "Can I accept this in good conscience?" "Would an outside, impartial observer accept it?" or "Is it all out in the open for all to see?"

The character of the organization you work for should be examined and periodically assessed. Some business organizations are operated, in whole or in part, for illegitimate objectives. The extent to which gangsters and hoodlums operate legitimate business as fronts is unknown, but the practice appears to be widespread in urban areas. Also, some persons consider the businesses they own as toys or playthings. They provide opportunities to manipulate people, to use power, and to enjoy the control of resources. And again, some owners use their businesses for tax-reducing or tax-manipulating purposes. It is doubtful that such objectives as these lend vitality to any organization. Enterprises of this sort seldom achieve distinction as stimulating, imaginative companies whose people are infused with a sense of the company's mission. To create a vibrant, pulsating organization, its leaders must communicate specific economic and social objectives to its members. To avoid becoming stagnant, the enterprise must seek and face live issues which can be framed into challenging patterns of objectives for all those associated with it.

Ethical issues keep occurring in all organizations, and their resolution must be compatible with the standards of ethics and morality sanctioned by society. The creative manager is aware of the moral and ethical dilemmas inherent in human endeavor and is resourceful in achieving goals without transcending these ethical and moral limits.

Professional Goals

Among the important goals for the creative manager is that of developing professional habits of thought and rules of conduct. Certain attitudes inherent in this concept can be of enormous help to you.

The idea of a profession is embodied to its fullest degree in such occupations as lawyer, doctor, teacher, or minister. A profession is thus a kind of occupation—a way of earning a living. But more than this, it is a way of contributing to the important needs of society. The earliest professions—teaching, preaching, or medicine—were distinguished from other occupations by the requirement of a formal education, which reflected the existence of a body of knowledge that the professional person had to possess. Some, such as ministers, went to special schools which were the forerunners of our modern liberal arts institutions. For many years lawyers acquired their right to practice by "reading law" under a practicing lawyer, a form of apprenticeship or internship. Medicine, too, linked formal study with internship in actual practice.

The early professions cultivated the ideal of service, placing remuneration below service in their list of priorities. Payment to teachers, ministers, and even attorneys and doctors was often "in kind"—the client gave goods or work rather than money in return for the professional's services. The professional was an independent practitioner who had a direct relationship with each client and who was usually more concerned about the client's needs than the method of compensation.

Over the years much has changed. While many of the attitudes and ideals of the basic professions remain in evidence, the manifest conditions of carrying out professional work are vastly different than the earlier models suggest. One major difference is that many professionals, even those from the basic traditional areas, no longer work as independent practitioners on a fee-for-advice basis. They work for organizations that pay them salaries. Hence, they have to work hard to maintain the fiction of independence while they are in fact subordinates in a complex organization.

A second difference is that they have been joined by a host of other occupational groups calling themselves professions: engineers, accountants, nurses, arbitrators, actuaries, and many others. In addition, there are the sub-professions, occupations such as salesperson and personnel manager. It is natural that many seek professional status in view of the high social position and other rewards society has conferred upon those in the traditional professions.

The earmarks of the traditional professions include (1) prescribed educational requirements reflecting a body of organized knowledge and expertise, (2) a system of examinations and licensing to obtain peer and governmental approval to practice, (3) a client relationship emphasizing the controlled use of specialized knowledge and a commitment to ideals of service, (4) payment by fees from clients, and (5) codes of ethical conduct and self-policing by members of the professions. Holding up the managerial occupations against this set of criteria indicates that they fit only the first criterion well.

There is a body of knowledge capable of being passed along through formal education. However, there is no general system of licensing, although some related groups such as psychologists or certified public accounts have a certification or licensing procedure. Licensing through examinations was attempted in Great Britain but was ultimately abandoned. There is no general control of entry to managerial positions through the apparatus of professionalism.

With respect to the client relationship, there is some applicability in the realm of *ad hoc* management consultants. Most managers work for organizations as full-time employees. Full-time employment is on a salary or a salary and bonus basis, and only outside consultants or members of boards of directors are remunerated by fees.

Management does not have a comprehensive code of behavior for all managers. However, many subgroups among managers and technicians have adopted ethical codes with some degree of success. Examples are: public relations officials, accountants, engineers, purchasing agents, and in some cases, personnel directors. These partial efforts are worth noting. In general, however, they lack the means of enforcement because the groups are not effectively organized for enforcement and do not usually receive support from government units.

Although management is not a sufficiently cohesive group to achieve the status of a full profession, there are several attributes inherent in the concept of professionalization which can serve as goals for the creative manager. The ultimate goal of complete professionalization is remote, and for purposes of career development, unnecessary. Instead, creative managers may usefully incorporate the basic attitudes that underlie professional behavior into their own day-to-day practice of management.

Let us now review these key attitudes.

First comes the notion of service. The service orientation implies that you are doing more than merely holding a job, working for money, or putting in time. It implies that your services are based on special skills or knowledge not readily available to others and that the recipients of such services cannot always judge for themselves the quality of the services rendered or know exactly what services are needed in a given situation.

Second, monetary awards are treated as secondary to service motivations. Professionals expect to be well paid, but their first thought is to provide competent and specialized service.

Third, professionals are aware that they will ultimately be judged by other professionals. Clients may express likes or dislikes, feelings or reactions, and may experience or fail to experience benefits, but they cannot directly judge the professional's technical capabilities in the same way as his fellow professionals. Therefore creative managers listen to other managers whom they respect and from whom they can learn.

Fourth, a key attitude is the acceptance of the possibility and the consequences of mistakes or failure. At least part of the time, professionals accept substantial risk, albeit with some estimate of the probabilities of failure.

Fifth is the recognition that professional status is earned by specific practices and not by the mere use of a title or letters after one's name. Results count the most in building a "professional" reputation.

Sixth, professionals try to give more than they receive and emphasize helping others to do the best job possible. They avoid the "what's in it for me" attitude, doing more than they are paid to do.

Seventh, professionals espouse attitudes of openness, inquiry, intellectual curiosity, and investigation. They are skeptical of sham and pretense. They are realists, but are not cynics. The hallmark of professional persons is the fact that they have goals. They know what they want to accomplish and whether or not their goals are realistic.

Eighth, professionals take a personal interest in their clients, the central focus of their work, but they exercise a certain neutrality and objectivity, and an independence of judgment. This leads to accepting full responsibility for their decisions and their advice and to having the courage to give the client unpopular or divergent advice.

Ninth, there is a great deal of self-discipline in the life of professionals. They work hard. They subject themselves to ethical constraints, and pay attention to the relations of their profession with other professions. They live in a world of continuous exposure to take criticism from clients and colleagues.

Tenth, professionals take a long view. They see problems in relation to each other and to the big picture. They take an interest in getting the right problem properly defined and out on the table.

Eleventh, professionals communicate and disseminate findings for the benefit of others. They share ideas and findings with others.

The attitude and values of the professionally oriented creative manager flourish best in the newer types of open, adaptive, flexible organizations that encourage meaningful participation on the part of its members. In the tight-ship bureaucracy, it is harder, though not altogether impossible, to apply the insights of professionalism.

Specific Goals for the Creative Manager

It is possible here to suggest only a few specific personal goals that will particularly help you in your work and in your career.

Getting to know what you need to know. This is difficult, for persons or situations may block you from obtaining the information you need. You can trust the grapevine, the rumor mill, which is fairly accurate much of the time. However, this unofficial source has the drawback that you can't act with certainty on rumor. Use it to find out where to look for hard facts you need. Attack the blocker by demanding what you need to know. Don't waste time trying to get information you don't need and have no use for. Establish long-term official and unofficial information sources. Protect the confidentiality of all your sources. Be frank in admitting what you do not know. Read and observe widely, far beyond the limits of your own particular specialty. Realize that much anxiety stems from not knowing what you should know and that learning is a great antidote for anxiety.

Preparing for your next job. This poses a dilemma, for there is good reason to concentrate mainly on the job you are doing now. The trick is to do the job you have now but use it to learn and observe what the next job entails. If it is a promotion, you should not try to hide your goals of obtaining it. Neither should you give this your only attention, as though there were no other goals.

Accept and use the presence of competition and conflict. They are part of the fun of being in a dynamic organization. Emphasize their constructive aspects and benefits; play down their negative overtones. Extreme, undisciplined competition and conflict can involve costs you can't afford. Lose necessary arguments gracefully. Fight tough battles fairly and in a gentlemanly way.

Enjoy serendipity. This concept refers to unsought benefits or consequences that can be turned to your advantage. It is a gift or art to discover the serendipity in ordinary events. Almost every event or act has more than one result, so you have to search for the extra dividends. Try to get more than one payoff for everything you do. Learning leads to serendipity—the discovery by chance or sagacity of the unsought benefit.

CHAPTER
3

How Strategies
Work for You

By choosing objectives, you have taken the first step in determining the activities you deem appropriate for your organization and for yourself. It is, however, necessary to examine the strategic factors inherent in the choice and pursuit of objectives. All managerial action reflects strategies designed to attain desired ends. The selection of strategies and their wise use in the organizational setting is a challenge to creative managers, setting them apart from those who are less imaginative in their approach to management.

In the course of your work, you pursue simultaneously a number of strategies to attain multiple, complex ends. You have overall, grand strategies for problems of continuing importance, and still other short-run strategies for the tasks to be done in a day or a week. As with multiple objectives, the problem is to relate the strategies to each other so as to minimize their conflicts and discrepancies and form a coherent pattern.

Strategic Behavior

Strategy is the word used to denote the actions managers take to achieve success for organizational or personal goals in a competitive and uncertain environment. Strategies are based on actual or probable actions of others, such as rivals, market competitors, suppliers, customers, employees, or governmental units.

Strategy includes an awareness of goals, the unpredictability and uncertainty of events, and the need to take into account the probable or actual behavior of others, principally opponents.

Strategies differ from plans and goals in their deliberate focus on winning an advantageous position over an opponent or in relation to others. Strategies are calculated to prevent or counteract actions of opponents, whereas plans usually specify direct goals and a consistent, orderly means for attaining them. Strategies comprise a fundamental part of planning, and the planning process is employed in the development of strategies. A strategy may be regarded as a special kind of plan that includes the concept of an opponent. Strategies consist of related actions, plans, and decisions designed to implement specific objectives. Elements of unpredictability, chance, risk, incomplete knowledge, extraneous influences, and the sheer complexity of an organization's operations constitute both a source of opportunity and of insecurity for the executive. The purposeful manager picks strategies that help establish advantageous relationships with the socio-economic environment in which action occurs, thereby reducing risk and insecurity.

The selection and implementation of strategies requires the use of conceptual, observational, and analytical skills. Strategies vary in quality and appropriateness for meeting demands on the organization. Therefore the executive finds that practicing these skills under dynamic, constantly changing conditions is helpful.

Strategies and Problem Solving

Strategies are needed not only for the pursuit of objectives but also for problem solving. Problems that go unsolved do so because managers are unable or unwilling to employ the strategies necessary to bring about their solution.

For every problem you need a strategy. But first you have to know what your real problems are and have a sense of the priorities by which your problems are related. Finally, you have to define your problem in operational terms, accurately, and in such a way as to help you find a working strategy that will solve it.

Just as problems are ranged in an order of priority, so too are the various strategies appropriate for meeting them. Strategies range from very broad, long-run ones to very simple and specific ones. It is important to temper the strategy to fit the problem. You don't want to stop a nosebleed with a tourniquet around your neck.

Defining your actual problems is not easy since they often lie beneath the surface and are not readily apparent. In this category are general long-range problems such as that of achieving a career goal. The farther away the result, the easier it is to put off thinking about it and to get caught up in more mundane, day-to-day pressures. Also, in the category of hidden problems are those concerning human relations. Conflicts between people are difficult to handle because the motivations of individuals lie beneath the surface.

Yet even after you thoughtfully recognize a problem area, it is easy to be fatalistic and to think that matters will take care of themselves. While confidence, optimism, and buoyancy of outlook are assets, one cannot live in an ivory tower. And though the future holds many uncertainties over which you have little or no control, it is realistic to do some creative forward planning. Thus broad, long-range problems should be analyzed in strategic terms that are appropriately broad and long range. They are, of course, subject to adjustment and change as you go along. No strategy will endure for all time, fixed and unswerving. The very essence of strategy is a continuous adjustment of tactical applications.

Your priorities thus lie along a time dimension and scales of urgency and magnitude. Focusing on these elements will help you devise a range of available strategies encompassing the present and the future. But to devise the proper strategies, you need to get each problem accurately defined.

Your definition of the problem significantly determines the nature of the answer (a strategy) you develop. For example, if you face excessive absenteeism among a group of your employees, you need a strategy for combating this problem. But the problem may be defined in several ways. One is that discipline is lax and tighter rules with tough enforcement are needed. This definition leads to a strategy of crackdown on rules, increased monitoring of behavior, and policies of swift punishment of offenders.

Another definition of the problem is that effective motivation of the absentee is lacking. This leads to a strategy of closer observation of the subordinates and their working conditions, an effort to learn what affects their decisions, a study of the objective conditions causing their behavior, and a reexamination of your relations with them as their supervisor. Ultimately, a strategy of greater freedom and responsibility and reeducation or better communications might result.

The Strategic Factor

A certain element of opportunism is embodied in the formulation and use of strategies. This element denotes the arena in which action must take place so that objectives may be achieved.

The attainment of objectives requires an ongoing decision process which in turn involves a search for strategic factors. These strategic factors are those whose control, in the right form and at the right time and place, will establish a new system or set of conditions which meets the intended purpose.

The strategic factor is in effect a limiting factor in the sense that for effective decision making it has to be discovered. Once isolated, this strategic factor redefines the purpose and focus of the action. It is the limiting (strategic) factor which the decision maker needs to change to secure the result he wants.

Suppose you have a work team that is not accomplishing its task on time or in the desired manner. To take action, you will need to isolate the strategic factor (or factors) which impede the team's progress. You examine the objective environment—the physical, biological, social, emotional, moral, and organizational elements in the situation. You then apply your understanding of historical developments, current facts, and personal experience to the selection of the strategic factors which need to be changed or controlled. Let us say you discover technical incompetence on the part of one team member. This then becomes your focus of decision and action. This strategic factor is a limiting factor because it is crucial and because it narrows the range of actions you will then take.

Strategic factors may consist of physical, tangible elements—such as equipment, tools, or facilities—or of social, psychological, or organizational processes. These latter areas are complex and hence the most difficult to find and utilize. The success of your problem solving and decision making depends heavily upon your ability to size up a situation by finding the strategic factor in which major change depends.

Pareto's law is useful here. It holds that a high percentage of your effort, time, and attention is demanded by a small percentage of cases. Ninety percent of the absenteeism in an organization may occur among 20 percent of the employees. And perhaps 80 percent of your strategy determination effort applies to 20 percent of your problems. The trick is to recognize the unique or difficult matters that need special attention where strategy is concerned.

Explicit and Implied Strategies

Strategies that underlie managerial action are not always overt or consciously adopted. Many explicit strategies are chosen deliberately through careful planning and extensive thought. But others are indirectly and subtly implied by observable behavior. Often the strategic implications of a given action or decision do not become apparent until after the action is taken.

All organizations and executives have strategies whether they make them explicit or not. Implied strategies exist in all courses of action or inaction. Deliberate strategies, however, are often shielded from view, since their revelation to or perception by others might limit or destroy their value. Restricted or implied strategies may become known, and hence become explicit strategies, after observers take note of behavior patterns and deduce the strategies from them.

Both explicit and implied strategies require continuous adjustments dictated by changes in the situation. No single strategy can succeed all the time and in all situations. No set of strategies remains fixed, for the essence of strategic thinking is to cope with actual and potential change. Factors that enter into original strategies undergo continual change. Consequently, the creative manager keeps reviewing, revising, and adapting his strategies to fit changing conditions.

Part of this change, and an important part, is in the relationship between explicit and implied strategy. The manager who attempts to keep both kinds of strategy under surveillance for purposes of modification is better off than one who leaves such matters to chance.

Personal Strategies

Your participation in organizational strategies will generally be in conjunction with other managers, through joint planning efforts, project teams, committees, or other groups. Your role in organizational strategies is affected by the work of others, and by constraints and opportunities inherent in the organization's way of operating. The nature of the environment, problems of the industry, and a host of internal factors determine the precise nature of organizational strategies.

By contrast, your personal strategies belong to you alone. You alone can devise them. You apply them to your tasks and relationships within an organizational setting, but only you can determine your goals and the ways of attaining them. You need to select and follow strategies for many reasons, not all of which are entirely clear to you or to others. Sometimes you may be unaware of the strategic implications of your own behavior; at other times you may be sharply calculating in the adoption of a strategy.

Understanding personal strategies requires a knowledge of human motivation and of psychological and sociological aspects of human conduct as they apply to you. You are, after all, an emotional as well as rational being. You are a thinking animal, but an imperfect one. You act both according to what you know and to what you feel. You have inner drives, needs, ambitions, and fears. You thrive in environments that reinforce your feelings of security and the needs for affiliation and being wanted. Hostile or uncertain environments may either make you fearful and unable to act or evoke your best abilities to meet the challenges. These inner drives, aspirations, and motivations keep you going, at least until an outwardly respectable or inwardly satisfying level of accomplishment is attained.

Many of your important needs are either satisfied or frustrated by the working environment. Therefore you design strategies to help you (1) alter your environment so that it is more to your liking and provides more of the net satisfactions you feel are desirable; (2) defend yourself against hostile, excessively demanding, or threatening elements; and (3) derive from the environment certain levels of material, social, psychological, and spiritual well-being.

An executive's personal strategies do not necessarily serve himself alone. Many are good for the organization. If you can persuade others that the strategies you prefer are in the best interests of your organization, department, or group, your strategies will be less likely to meet with opposition. The test of what is good for an organization, however, is uncertain, so that executives who seek to endorse private strategies with the cloak of organizational welfare may find others skeptical. Some executives may delude themselves into believing the nonexistent unselfish motives they declare. On the other hand, many personal strategies are congruent with or will not hinder the needs of the organization, which after all are numerous and complex. The dividing line between personal and organizational strategies is not always clear, and the two types are subtly interrelated.

Personal strategies clearly not in the long-run interests of the organization or the individual should be employed only in the most extreme or unusual cases, if ever. Vicious strategies of revenge, hostility, or attack on others, or those which would generally be deemed unethical, should be avoided.

Power Strategies

Power strategies are designed to reinforce or improve your position in the organization in competition with colleagues or rivals. The hierarchical structure poses the challenge of climbing it, and social and organizational forces press you to go as far as you can. Progress is widely defined as moving upward in the organization's levels of authority, power, and influence. One who accepts the challenge of climbing the hierarchy needs strategies focused on this goal. Some executives are more opportunistic than others, awaiting rather than creating goal-reinforcing events. Others are energetic and determined in their efforts to advance and to acquire power.

Aspiration levels are a key element in the drive for power. Some aspire to power for its own sake, finding it exhilarating to hold a large empire. Others may seek power to accomplish unselfish aims for the good of society. Still others reject power entirely as an instrument for fulfilling their life values. Power may come to those who do not aspire to it, but more typically it lodges with those who have aggressively sought it.

Power strategies may be positive or negative. Positive strategies favor the executive's goal directly by strengthening his position relative to others. Negative strategies reduce or dilute the power or position of others in relation to himself. Both positive and negative strategies may be within or without the sphere of ethical conduct. Unethical strategies ultimately exact a heavy price from those willing to use them. In the case of negative power strategies, the executive faces serious questions about the extent to which selected strategies may hurt others.

Communications activity, management styles, and interaction patterns are all instruments of power strategies. By a strategy of selectivity in communications upward, downward, or laterally, for example, one keeps adverse information from hurting. By controlling what's communicated, one may tip the balance in one's favor in key decisions. Management styles can be developed to abet strategies reinforcing power and influence. If the strategy is one of rapid, aggressive advance in the system, a hard-driving, hard-nosed management style can help, especially if the opponents' styles are quiet, patient, and careful.

Interaction patterns are also important. Each day executives make decisions about whom to contact, whom not to contact, and how much time to spend with each person with whom they interact. The strategy of advancement in power, influence, and position requires constant interaction with those who can contribute the most to the executive's goals. This strategy, of course, can be overdone, and quality of the content of the interaction time is also crucial. But the key factor is spending time with important persons in important places. Here are several examples of power strategies:

Divide and conquer; establish and attain subgoals.
Strike while the iron is hot.
Conduct a massive offensive; concentrate energies, resources.

Counterattack wherever possible.

Do what you want and let others attack.

In union there is strength; develop strategic coalitions.*

Ego-Reinforcing Strategies

Some important strategies serve to build up strong self-images of the executive. By following such strategies, executives who have tendencies to feel inadequate or uncertain about their roles in the organization may derive reinforcement of a feeling of importance and being needed. An example of this kind of strategy is the executive who keeps excessively busy, works too hard at his job, and seldom "lets down" in the drive for excellence, perfection, and accomplishment. This type of executive undergoes self-imposed pressures, which reflect his own patterns of self-organization. To some degree this strategy is self-defeating because the excessive activity interferes with creativity, planning, and the development of job perspective. It creates tensions among colleagues and subordinates and causes the executive to take shortcuts that conserve time at the expense of satisfactory human relations on the job.

Other ego-reinforcing strategies are less difficult because they reflect patterns of behavior widely accepted as part of the folklore of organizations. For example, consider the strategy surrounding the creation and use of status symbols. Having a large office, carpeted floor, draperies, paintings on the walls, and private secretaries when others in the hierarchy are excluded from having them helps strengthen executive egos by providing physical evidence of the importance of one's position in the organization.

Here are some strategies that illustrate the ego-reinforcing types:

Keep one jump ahead of the other fellow.

Keep on sawing wood.

Big oaks from little acorns grow.

---

*Power strategies are currently receiving much attention. See Michael Korda, *Power* (New York: Random House, 1975); Robert J. Ringer, *Winning Through Intimidation* (Los Angeles: Los Angeles Book Publishers, Inc., 1973). For a compendium of tactics see Richard H. Buskirk, *Handbook of Managerial Tactics* (Boston: Cahners Publishing Co., Inc., 1976).

Sow seed on fertile ground.
Try something new only when success is certain.
Capitalize on apparent defeat.

Work Strategies

Work strategies pertain to the way executives relate to their work and responsibilities in the organization. They represent the modes of action that executives select in order to shape their relationships to jobs, careers, and to organizations. Work strategies may, of course, be combined or used in conjunction with other strategies.

Your time is an important asset, and the way you use it is to a large degree a matter of discretion, so it can be a part of your strategy formulations. Thus one strategy for working against a decision you dislike is simply not to carry out the decision. By not doing the work or by doing it wrong, you can delay or even destroy the results. You can even avoid undue penalty by rationalizing or explaining the delays. In any case, the punishment—usually a reprimand—is bearable, though this does not mean that the strategy is a wise or an appropriate one.

Loyalty provides another element of work strategy. Organizations tend to place a high value on member loyalty. Executives expect loyalty of their subordinates. Therefore the executive and the subordinate are in a position to bargain with the organization or with their superiors to get the best price for their loyalty. People can adjust the degree of loyalty according to their opinions about the extent to which the organization or their superiors merit it. The question of loyalty could be a deliberately chosen strategy, but more often it emerges out of the need to choose among competing interests. For example, an executive may travel away from his office more than necessary. By becoming overly active in professional, civic, or trade associations, ties with the organization are loosened.

Work strategies can have other positive results. Others tend to appreciate and admire those who are skillful in their work and who use good judgment and balance in their approach to the quality and amount of their work. Most tasks can be done in a variety of ways, giving the executive a wide area of discretion in performing work. Good work generates confidence on the part of one's supervisor, tending to relax tight reins of control. Doing work with style and flair sets one apart from pedestrian colleagues.

As with other types of strategies, work strategies vary in the degree of subtlety they represent. Some are relatively passive, not being readily apparent to others; for example,

Trial balloons—"feelers" to avoid rejection.
Bide your time—use strategic delays.
Let time be a great healer.
Let things get worse; they'll get better later on.
Avoid decisive engagements, especially if your case is weak.

Other strategies are more subtle and calculating, such as:

Cooptation: absorb new elements into a situation to avert or dilute threats.
Tell only what you wish others to hear for a purpose.
Loaded deck; obtain inside information.
Camel's head in the tent—make a small beginning.
Bore from within: Use a Trojan horse, find the opponent's Achilles' heel, use unwilling allies' cat's paw strategy.
Create red tape: confuse and delay.
Draw red herrings across the trail.

Career Strategies

Many job holders give little thought to the planning of their careers. In fact these people often do not recognize that they have careers. It is enough for them to find and hold a job. Job changes are problems of immediate importance rather than definite steps in a long-range plan of career development.

Professional persons, trained specialists, or artists are the prototype of career followers. The notion has also become very important in the world of management. A career reflects a long-term commitment to an occupational work interest, to be pursued by continuous learning, growth, and development, quite probably as an independent practitioner or in connection with service to a number of organizations in succession. The idea of a career also implies that as people grow older, their careers should be advancing.

Indifference to career planning is caused not only by limited economic alternatives for the individual but also by uncertainty as to what occupational activities best fit the individual's capabilities. Young people are under great pressure to make an early career choice and not to fail at it. Schools, parents, and counselors are available to help, but at the same time, they are part of the pressure system. Our socio-economic culture does not encourage delay, exploration, and experimentation among youth in regard to occupational decisions.

Another reason for career indifference is that some people are content with their status quo. Their level of ambition or aspiration is low. The manager who is indifferent to advancement can often get by on a job-to-job or day-to-day basis. But the professional manager with creative impulses tries to envision a career path over time as successive job opportunities arise. An awareness of career objectives helps one take the best advantage of the job decisions that inevitably come to the more able individuals in society.

A career choice need not be a lifetime commitment, but a general career plan provides a way of recognizing deviations as temporary and useful guidelines for getting back on the main road once the byways have been explored. For example, a young black graduate of a business school traveled in Europe for a year on a fellowship. He then returned to school and earned his MBA degree, working part-time for a number of excellent companies during this period. After graduation, he joined a large bank in New York City. After two years of banking, he left the bank to become project director in a nonprofit educational association devoted to working with problems of racial discrimination. But he kept this job in perspective by keeping in mind his long-term goals:

> When I have completed my assignment with this educational group, I know in a general way what I want to do with the rest of my life. I want to pursue a career with a major financial institution in a speciality area such as real estate, municipal financing, or commodities trading. I expect such a career to provide me with a continuous learning experience, the opportunity to acquire

wealth, the ability to contribute to the well-being of others, and finally the power to have a positive influence in the community I live in. Although I am not yet sure of the precise course my future will follow, I am already beginning to have a clear idea of the steps I must take in order to achieve my personal goals.*

It should be recognized that for many people, if not most, a career does not follow an orderly, measured, paced progression of changes. It is often desirable to try unusual alternatives, to learn by exploring, and to take advantage of opportunities that unexpectedly present themselves. Nevertheless, it is desirable to have a well thought through general plan against which such opportunities can be examined. Occasionally one sees an individual following a zigzag career path with a hard to discern rationale. It may seem to lead everywhere or nowhere. We call this the career maverick. Career mavericks usually know where they want to go ultimately, but their philosophy leads them to adopt unorthodox routes to their goal. Primarily they are eager to seize upon unusual learning opportunities. It is important for the maverick to make sure that each job taken is actually a challenging and worthwhile experience, rather than a reflection of aimless drifting.†

Career mavericks often do things in an unusual way, such as quitting one job before they have found or decided upon the next. When changing jobs, it is important to avoid the appearance of aimless drifting, or rapid job hopping. The way to do this is to envision the accomplishments possible within each job taken. When those accomplishments are attained, one senses a dead end and is ready to move on. The aggressive, upwardly mobile manager can move up in the same organization; the maverick does it by broken field running maneuvers among a number of different organizations. If your record shows too many jobs in too many different places for too short a time, you had

---

*Lloyd M. Arrington, "Why Minorities Shun Management Careers and Why They Shouldn't," *MBA: The Master in Business Administration*, January 1975, p. 17.

†The word "maverick," used to describe independent personalities and stray cattle, is taken from the name of Samuel Augustus Maverick, Texas pioneer and politician noted for his rugged individualism.

better be ready with a good explanation for the pattern when searching for another position.

A career strategy consists of long-range aims to use as benchmarks for progress together with action plans that will help you at each critical turning point. With careful planning, you can take the initiative in making changes so you will not have to be subject to someone else's whim or estimate of your capabilities. Don't abdicate your responsibilities to others by default.

The benchmarks you need include your progress along salary, responsibilities, and prestige dimensions at particular points in your life. These should over time be commensurate with your abilities, education, and growing experience. Also, if you become bored, tired, or disinterested in the work involved in a particular job, it is time to reassess where you are along your career path.

You will need substrategies to cover the continued need for additional formal education and the acquisition of significant experiences by apprenticeship to or sponsorship of key individuals from whom you can learn the most. You will also need a set of strategies covering the alliances you make, the cliques you join, and other associations, such as the committees you serve on.

One strategy familiar to many is changing back and forth from line to staff jobs. This is known as the ping-pong strategy. In using this strategy, stick mostly with the line positions if the upward sectors of administration and management are your goals.

When you've stopped learning or making a contribution to a job, it is time to change. The time span is usually about two years in your early jobs, and about five in a post such as department head or vice-president or president.

One of the more subtle strategies is to form the habit of making others around you look good, especially your boss. Cultivate and acquire a reputation as an innovator with a style that distinguishes you from the crowd.

You don't have to be afraid to be different. If someone cares that you are different, you may be in the wrong organization. Advancement comes with being noticed, and if you are like others, you won't be in the running for opportunities that arise. One economist has said, not entirely in jest, that neurotics have the best chance to get ahead, because they're noticed. Be visible is the strategy here; take part in things; don't hide your light under a bushel.

Another useful strategy is to find good advice and know when you need it. At critical turning points, you need information. There are many helpful sources and some not so helpful. Friends may not give you unbiased advice, but recruiters, search firms, and university contacts will.

Perhaps the central strategy is to make sure you do the job you are engaged to do. All other strategies are hollow unless you have given your best to the tasks at hand. Play on the company team until the time comes when it is clear that you have to depart. It is prudent to know one's self-interest but not to flaunt it in the faces of everyone else all the time.

Without some degree of career planning, you are at the mercy of what is offered to you by someone else. Good career planning develops alternatives that make you look better in the job you are in now. While planning one's career smacks of shrewdness and cold calculation, some degree of career management is an intelligent action. Central to this matter is the idea of understanding the organization you are in, knowing where you fit in the scheme of things in your particular organization, and knowing where you want to go.

All this takes a bit of self-study to compare your personality, temperament, outlooks, and philosophies with those of the organization you are in. Organizations vary in these dimensions, and you can be unhappy if you are a highly creative, restless, ambitious individual working for a plodding bureaucracy. Or, if your bag is security, safety, and steady results, you had better not work for a fledgling company trying to produce and market a new invention or one that is led by an eccentric inventor or pioneer.

Organizations go through developmental phases, so consider whether you want to be with a new organization, stressing entrepreneurship and risk, or whether you want to be in a more mature organization. Watch out, too, for the mature organization that may be about to slide downhill through stagnation. You also need to have a picture of the social skills demanded of a member of an organization. What are the risks of change or failure? Are there stiff rules, written and unwritten, to which conformity is expected? How does your organization value innovation and change? Are there unusual demands, such as long hours, excessive loyalty, sacrifice, pressure, and risk? Is the company decadent or vitalized? Is there management by control or by inspiration?

The above queries are susceptible mainly to subjective evaluation. You can assess on an objective basis the firm's standing in its industry, its profitability and profit potential, its balance sheet and other accounting data, and the reputations of its managers among other managers.

Your ultimate purpose in all this is to find what you want and to match the organization's characteristics, at least approximately, with your own. Your best strategies are those which come from a conscious effort to expand your awareness of self and others.

The Mid-Career Crisis

You have heard much these days about the mid-career crisis. While there are many critical turning points in your career, the one that hits at the mid-thirties may be the trickiest. Many managers in this age bracket suddenly become unnerved. They let their careers go flat or abandon them entirely.

Psychologists believe that the mid-career crisis is a reflection of profound changes in the individual's inner self and in one's relationship to the internal and external environments. Feelings of frustration, anger, and despair abound, partly due to the aging process. Often the individual experiences a reawakening of unresolved problems that occurred in the early stages of life. Guilt feelings arise that reflect ways in which conditions are not what they could have been if one had behaved better in the past. Awareness of death and one's inability to halt the aging process leads to frustration, bitterness, and hostility. People suffering in this way often go out of their way to destroy the vital parts of their lives—health, career, and marriage.

There are two common reactions to the mid-career crisis: fleeing from it all—a feeling of helplessness, withdrawal, and uselessness—or fighting back—finding ways to strengthen one's ability to face death, failures, and disappointments. This is an important time to reassess one's goals and the means available for attaining them. Career planning helps one cope with the mid-career crisis, but many need additional help in coming to terms with themselves. Help is available in the form of counseling and other therapeutic measures.

Many people, under pressure from parents and schools, choose careers too early, at an age when they do not have the experience and judgment to know what occupations are most congenial to them. In their mid-thirties, they see that it is too late to start the activities which they now think would have been right.

Yet careers once chosen do not have to be followed for all time. In modern society, there is much changing of careers in midstream, probably at the point of the mid-career crisis. Many persons now envision two or three distinct career programs for themselves, depending on opportunities and the feasibility of learning and securing the needed additional training. Universities and other kinds of schools are a valuable resource for programs, both credit and noncredit, designed to help adults stay current in their jobs or to develop new careers for themselves.

Lest you think that additional education and training are unsuitable as you advance in age, you should know that the world is full of *opsimaths*. This is a made-up word denoting those who undertake formal study late in life. Society holds the opsimath in high esteem.*

In sum, the matter of strategies is a critical factor in one's work and career. The selection of any strategy must be fitted carefully to the problem situation it is intended to change. The enormous variety of available strategies should be appraised in accordance with ethical standards as well as their projected outcomes.

---

*The word *opsimath* derives from the Greek. Now rare, the term was first used by an English writer in 1676, but learning late in life was then considered a disgrace, even a vice.

CHAPTER
4

Your Domain
and Others

In some organizations, the relationships among people are highly structured. That is, formal relationships are very important. In others, one finds relaxed and flexible ideas about interaction. To work effectively with others, every manager needs an understanding of the structural framework for decision making.

The way you work with other managers in your organization is an important factor in your success. This means more than merely getting along with your fellow managers, for harmonious relationships can exist without necessarily adding up to productive, effective effort. The nature of the organizational framework and the operating characteristics it makes possible influence your work by establishing basic relationships between you and other managers.

Formal and Informal Domains

One fundamental aspect of organization structure is the establishment and maintenance of domains. These formal and informal domains constitute a network of related systems and subsystems. Formal domains are deliberately built into the organization; informal domains consist of unofficial group and individual behavior patterns that augment and transcend the formal structures in which they occur.

Informal domains reflect the personalities and abilities of individuals, the needs of groups, and the web of verbal and symbolic communications. Formal domains, on the other hand, are tied to technologies, missions, objectives, logistics, plans, and the like. However, the two domain structures are closely intertwined, the formal being the base around which the informal emerges. The informal relationships may be regarded as an overlay on the basic formal structures.

The idea of domains implies territorial boundaries. Just as an organization erects boundaries around itself to maintain its identity, so also do the subunits of an organization develop boundaries. The domain over which you preside has an integrity of its own with which all its members are familiar and comfortable. Challenges to the cohesiveness of their domain are unsettling to group members. In working with your own subordinates, you manage your domain problems with the aid of authority and responsibility, key elements of the formal structure. In relating your domain and its activities to other domains, the informal aspects of organization, chiefly persuasion and negotiation, come into play. This presents both an opportunity and a problem for the creative manager. Problems stem from the difficulties of change, conflict, and coordination which lie at the boundaries of the various domains. Opportunities arise out of the need for structure in every situation you encounter. You can provide the structure rather than just let it evolve without direction or control. Your concept of the boundaries of your domain becomes a point of reference for observing the intrusions of others or the excursions of your staff.

Boundaries provide an organizational unit with a sense of solidarity and importance. The unit acquires visibility, an image or identity that gives focus and meaning to its efforts. Boundaries also indicate important information about insiders and outsiders. This provides a way to judge the legitimacy of formal transactions.

Boundary Spanners

It is important for you to identify the boundary spanners in your organizational unit as well as those in other units. You are the most important boundary spanner, and in your capacity as a leader and manager, you will be in frequent contact with the heads of other units which are also engaged in boundary-spanning functions.

Boundary-spanning activity is not only the province of the heads of organizational units, it can occur whenever any person's tasks and duties require contact and communication with another person across a unit's boundary. Your secretary, for example, is a channel of communication through which outsiders reach you. Your subordinates may be performing work which requires them to cross the boundaries of their units. Therefore it is important that you teach them how and when it is done. It is more than a technical skill; it requires knowledge and practice in the communication of policies, attitudes, and points of view.

The utility and effectiveness of boundaries depends on the idiosyncrasies, perceptions, and attitudes of individuals, which vary from one circumstance to another. For example, in some instances, managers may pretend that boundaries really don't exist or allege that they are made to be crossed. At other times, depending on evolving strategies, managers may give boundaries more significance than they deserve. Boundaries can be noticed or not, depending on the nature of the problem or decision being considered and on the intentions of the persons involved.

Highly bureaucratic organizations tend to place great stress on the importance of the boundaries of units, a fact which complicates the process of coordination. Boundaries thus intensify the formal aspects of organization. It is in the interplay of informal elements of organization that boundaries are ignored or readily transcended.

Strong, vertically oriented functional units, such as departments of marketing, production, finance, or engineering, provide examples of conditions in which boundaries are emphasized and coordination is difficult. On the other hand, organizations built around processes or projects underplay the role of boundaries and generate conditions in which both formal and informal linkages can more easily take place.

In many organizations, managers develop a high degree of parochialism with respect to their domains and their boundaries. That is, their view of the organization is limited in range and scope, so that their unit is seen as the most important center of activity. Even worse, managers may be chauvinistic, showing undue partiality or attachment to their unit, which they idealize and direct as though pursuing some great cause. The chauvinistic manager is likely to put the unit's welfare ahead of the welfare of the total organization.

For the creative manager, the establishment, maintenance, and defense of a domain is something of an art. There is a time to be aggressive and a time to be defensive about one's domain. Knowing these differing circumstances is one of the manager's primary responsibilities.

Domain Consensus

Considerable awareness of domains and their structure is a requisite of effective management, but domain management requires finesse. Too much domain consciousness produces undesirable effects, such as the intensification of bureaucratic rigidities, excessive conflict, jealousy, bickering, and defensive, self-serving attitudes. Yet some degree of order and structure must be maintained. On the other hand, too little concern about domains results in a flabby organization, producing uncertainty among those who have tasks to perform. Organization members, after all, do find security in the existence of domains.

The organization is able to survive and carry out its work because some degree of domain consensus is achieved. This is general, if temporary, agreement as to the nature of existing domains, their boundaries and missions, and their relationships to each other. But these domains are never static. They are constantly changing, sometimes gradually and at other times rapidly. By common consent, it is often possible to ignore a domain constraint for a short time. But as work continues, domains reassert themselves and new ones emerge.

Domain consensus entails agreement on both goals and the means for achieving them because the organization is an instrument by which managers achieve their purposes. An organization is not like a jigsaw puzzle in which the individual pieces have permanent contours and only one function and location in the total result. Rather, the functions and contours of each organizational unit are what its members make of them at any given time. In such a context, domain consensus evolves out of the give and take between people on the work scene, continuous negotiations and renegotiations, and habit and tradition. All domains are subject to continuous challenge, redefinition, disappearance, and recreation.

Because domain consensus is shifting and volatile and because certain parts of the organization compete with each other, domains overlap and impinge on each other. But it is not the domains themselves that jockey with each other for power and position, it is the managers who manipulate domains by initiating changes, acquiring resources, expanding their scope, and adjusting changes. As managers relate such changes to their own position, status, security, and complex social-psychological factors make their way through informal mechanisms into the formal system. Hence we witness the great game of "organizational politics" as managers play their roles in the competitive ebb and flow of domains.

Linkages Among Domains

Your domain is not an empire unto itself. It is inextricably woven into the web of the complex interrelationships and interdependencies of the organization structure.

Interrelationships concern less formal matters than interdependencies. One key to understanding interrelationships is to recognize that they center around the person involved. Another key is that people have considerable latitude in determining the character and duration of the interrelationships in which they participate. For example, a production manager, to some degree, has to handle public relations problems. But to have the staff public relations group closely supervise this activity poses problems. Therefore the staff managers must take a persuasive, selling approach in their relationship with the production department, and the production manager must learn to respond effectively to their guidance, ideas, and policies.

All line-staff problems fit this model of temporary, fluctuating, or problem-centered interrelationships and are subject to a wide latitude of choice with regard to their nature and duration. All interpersonal relationships, such as coalitions, task forces, committees, even coffee-drinking or friendship groupings, display these characteristics.

Interdependencies reflect some of the characteristics of such interrelationships but introduce more complex problems for creative managerial action. Interdependencies consist of linkages required by technologies, processes, and the expectations induced by formal organization structures. Any change in them requires overt consensus and sanction by those with the appropriate formal authority. In this area there is little latitude for discretionary judgments, since pressures for change are generated by technological, legal, or societal imperatives.

An example is provided by the practice of taking advantage of discounts for prompt payment of suppliers' invoices. The purchasing agent, the inventory manager, and the financial manager are linked in an interdependent system because the action of any of them can affect the results of the others. They are all dependent, however, on the kinds of discounts offered by outsiders (suppliers). They will also be constrained to maximize profit or minimize costs by finding the optimum set of decisions, possibly with the help of sophisticated operations research techniques from management scientists. Any changes in these interdependent linkages, therefore, would have to originate in major developments in financial technology, management science, or possibly in the organization's financial policies.

An important implication of this analysis is that the manager must accept the existence of interdependencies with equanimity, while at the same time being aware of opportunities for creative change. Moreover, the management of interdependencies may be enhanced by the skillful management of interrelationships, and vice versa. A marketing manager, for example, may wish to control and direct the training programs for salesmen. However, there is likely to be an extensive training activity managed by the personnel department. The marketing manager's sales training program can be developed in its interdependency with activities of the personnel department's program if the interrelationships between the two sets of managers are conducive to collaboration between the two domains.

Domain Congruence

Knitting domains into a fabric of effective working patterns is a problem of coordination. Cooperation, while desirable for many reasons, is not sufficient.

Coordination at the level of domains works in two dimensions—the horizontal and the vertical (unless hierarchy has been laid aside). Departmentalization tends to construct domains across the horizontal dimension, whereas the delegation of authority introduces a vertical dimension. This matrix of domains needs continuous attention from managers if coordinated efforts are to result.

The horizontal dimensions of the domain structure of an organization result in specialization of tasks, duties, and responsibilities. Each unit has a functional identity, whether line or staff. This identity is a rallying point for recruiting expertise into the organization, for the leader's morale-building efforts, and for the steady performance of necessary and desirable tasks and responsibilities. The unit also provides a focal point for the attention of higher managers who may intervene for purposes of direction, control, and evaluation of results.

The vertical dimension distributes delegated authority down and across the filaments of the structural web. The processes of delegation and accountability combine to legitimize the behavior in each domain and to give support and sanction to their managers.

The model just described, however, gives an undue impression of logic and exactitude. In reality, the various domains do not enjoy precisely measured vertical and horizontal bounds. Human beings are so constituted that no amount of fine tuning by managers can permanently constrain their vital life forces. As personal talents, values, beliefs, and experiences are applied to a formal structure, that structure acquires a patina analogous to that on fine silver long in use.

No amount of coordination, clarity of delegation, or tampering with written job descriptions can permanently eliminate some degree of overlapping and some degree of jurisdictional conflict among domains. Furthermore, overlapping and conflict have benefits as well as drawbacks. The benefits include the enjoyment and challenge of uncertainty, the greater assurance that key

functions will not be omitted or mishandled, greater resourcefulness in problem solving, and greater chances for innovativeness
and creativity to occur. The drawbacks include the costs of dupli-
cated efforts, difficulties associated with ambiguities, and possibilities for buck-passing and avoidance of responsibility.

We can summarize these points by saying that the creative
manager develops a sense of the fitness of things concerning
domains. He is not afraid to acknowledge that domains exist,
change, interact with other domains, and have complex dimensions. We can call this the manager's "domain consciousness."
Clearly a manager with an unduly rigid domain consciousness
inhibits growth, flexibility, and problem solving. Also, a manager
with little or no domain consciousness is bereft of valuable
sources of stability, support, and rationality.

One's colleagues and subordinates expect some degree of domain dominance by groups and individuals but not to the point
where narrow, parochial attitudes toward one's domain erect
barriers to serving the larger goals of the enterprise. A familiar
example can be found in attitudes expressed toward empire
building. This phrase automatically evokes connotations of op-
probrium from many but admiration from some. Those who are
not involved in the action will be its critics; those who benefit are
prone to applaud. Empire building motivated solely by personal
aggrandizement cannot easily be condoned. Empire building for
achieving greater effectiveness, social betterment, or economic
contributions reflects more readily accepted motives. But the
two kinds of motivation are not easily discerned or separated,
since empire builders gain personally as their organizations gain.

Examples of Domain Conflicts

The significance of domains can best be illustrated by an analysis
of three common types of domain problems widely found in both
profit and nonprofit organizations: departmental structures,
line-and-staff-unit authority, and headquarters-field conflicts.

DEPARTMENTS

Departments are usually organized along functional lines, although they may have geographical or purely technical dimen-

sions. The department consists of a major function such as marketing, finance, or production, together with all the logical subfunctions which give the unit a coherent mission to perform. The organizing principle is to group logical functions and activities together, provide a designation that identifies the unit and its activities, and delegate all the responsibilities to a department head. Thus the purpose, the people, and the identity are linked together as major contributors to organizational goals.

Clearly there is nothing sacred about a departmental structure, although some persons may behave as though there is. Since it is a tool to achieve given ends, it may be improved or discarded. Yet once this domain has been created, there are those in the organization who will fight to preserve it to the end, and there are also those who will stop at nothing to attack or destroy it. Therefore representatives and occupants of the domain may be defensive at times, and aggressive at other times. They forge emotional bonds of loyalty to the departmental image and to colleagues they admire.

A further problem with departmental domains is to recognize that they must steer a steady course between the two extremes of autonomy and dependence. The department has impulses to be totally independent, to concentrate on its own destiny, and to protect its own interests first. But it is also ambivalent about this, recognizing at the same time a strong need for linkages with the rest of the organization from which it draws support, resources, information, and a *raison d'être*. Therefore either extreme is impractical, and the course of events will find the department under different pressures at different times.

The role of department head is crucial to the success of the departmental structure. Weak leadership, poor management, and lack of knowledge may cause the department head to lose the confidence of subordinates, and what is equally bad, the confidence of the heads of other domains. The department head must create cohesion, loyalty, and high morale among group members while at the same time maintaining linkages with other groups and keeping the department afloat in the complex activities reaching beyond the domain's boundaries.

Department heads are important figures in an organization. They represent their groups to the rest of the organization, are the groups' chief spokesmen, and are pivotal factors in the success of both formal and informal communications. They are the approved pathways by which communications are funneled upward and downward in the organization. Thus they are often caught in the middle of countervailing pressures and demands.

Subordinates expect department heads to represent their interests in contentions and struggles with other domains, both inside and outside the organization. They expect the department head to help them get their share of benefits and rewards from the organization. When any issue is being faced, the department head is forced to make choices either favoring or not favoring the expectations of subordinates. The department head can't win all the time for one side or the other may believe that it has lost something in any argument or problem.

Thus department heads may sometimes become scapegoats. They have to accept the blame if things go wrong. They may even be blamed by everyone—by those higher up as well as those below, and for opposite reasons. Subordinates by their performance can make them or break them.

LINE AND STAFF

Conflicts between line and staff units provide a second example of the problems of domain management and domain consciousness. Whenever there is a differentiation of this type, emphasizing differences in the authority of the two kinds of units, there is likely to be rivalry, tension, and misunderstandings. In the line-staff domains, the line domain dominates over the staff specialists, whose work includes functions ultimately belonging to the line. An organization usually creates staff units as a means of bringing highly specialized experts into the organization to assist the line with more generalized responsibilities. Thus a staff domain cuts horizontally across all the line domains and some of the other staff domains. An example is the personnel department, whose activities affect all employees. Thus differences and conflicts are deliberately structured into the system in the belief that the benefits of specialization will be greater than the problems provoked.

While there are a number of ways to reduce tensions and conflict, it is well to recognize the difficulties involved. Some studies show that after line-staff managers work together over periods of time, they achieve an accommodation to each other which enables them to get along better. Some organizations rotate upward-mobile managers between line and staff domains to round out their experience and enrich their insights and skills. While this can be helpful in increasing understanding and reducing tension, it has a built-in fallacy, namely that the specialization required is not after all very technical, so that line people can be rotated into the staff jobs. The success of this move may vary from one kind of organization to the next. In general, staff people can probably convert to line jobs more readily than the other way around. The best staff work is not likely to be performed by those only partly qualified but willing to learn.

In the development of your career, you should consider the extent to which you would attempt such rotation between line and staff domains. If you can convince your superiors that you can do the jobs in both domains with some benefit to the company as well as to yourself, you may be able to gain invaluable experience. On the other hand, you have to guard against undertaking some part of the work for which you have insufficient aptitude or interest and therefore a substantial chance of failure.

HEADQUARTERS AND FIELD

One set of important domain problems in many organizations is the classic headquarters-field problem. This problem occurs in organizations having a central office of line and staff people who supervise a rather large network of subsidiaries, divisions, or other units that are more or less widely separated geographically. A sales manager in the corporate office with a network of regional and local sales forces spread all over the United States is an example.

The essence of the headquarters-field problem is that the managers at the center find it difficult to know what is going on out in the field. Therefore they tend to exert strong controls, adding to the bureaucratic machinery and increasing the red tape. Field personnel tend to resent too much control and too close supervision. Field personnel become distrustful of the central corporate domain because they think it is out of touch with the realities of the local situation. The central group, on the other hand, suspects that those in the field are getting away with too much and are doing things they shouldn't be.

The central office by necessity must get its information by demanding reports from the field or by sending coordinators or other managers out to inspect the field activities. Field managers come to resent the paperwork and to regard the home office representative as a spy or a busybody. One way out of these dilemmas is to decentralize authority by making field units into autonomous groups and evaluating them by their results by a rather harsh "put-up-or-shut-up" attitude, when the autonomous units complain about lack of help from the central office. So it becomes a question of balance to unite and coordinate the field and headquarters domains—a balance between effective control and adequate assistance on the part of the central office group, with sufficient autonomy in field operations to meet local conditions and special situations.

Organizational Politics

For many, the term politics carries bad connotations. The infamous Watergate disclosures of the mid-1970s caused a severe decline in confidence and respect for politicians. Nevertheless, political behavior is a reality in both our cultural and organizational life. It can be a constructive or destructive force, but good or bad, it is a necessity of governance if society is to endure.

To examine political elements in organizational behavior is to acknowledge the presence of power, leadership, and constituencies competing for influence and resources. Much of the behavior called "politics" in organizations has to do with power conflicts between domain structures and the managers representing them. It is evoked, too, by the strivings of organization members to achieve the fulfillment of various kinds of needs.

At least four postulates about organizational politics can be specified. The first is that no organization is devoid of politics or politicians in both the invidious and constructive senses. This is because inherent in the system is the opportunity for persons wishing to do so to advance in pay, status, and responsibility. Also, inherent in the individual are impulses to achieve security, power, influence, recognition, and status. The organization thus becomes the framework of the political processes by which both the organization and its members gain their objectives.

A second postulate is that not all "politics" on the part of organization members is bad. Managers need not fear political behavior when observed in others, nor should they fear to use it judiciously themselves. It becomes invidious when excessive, when selfish motivation outstrips organizational welfare, and when little or no benefit is obtained relative to its costs. Politics is constructive when it results in competitive forces which bring out the best in people, tests ideas through persuasion and analysis, and develops leaders.

A third postulate is that the deliberate, calculated use of "politics" as an instrument of one's advancement must be subtle. It works best in low gear. It requires special skills and understandings if it is to be used adroitly. Overkill is easy, and it repels one's colleagues. Accordingly, politics is one of the several applied arts of organizational behavior, and should never be heavy-handed.

A fourth postulate, related to the other three, is that the politically sensitive manager becomes identified as an involved person in the organization. He shows himself to be aware of domains, constituencies, pressures, changes, relationships, ongoing problems. Hiding or running from political realities is as unrealistic as overkill is ridiculous. Very few significant decisions are made in an organization that are devoid of political aspects. Every manager has been dealt a set of political cards which have to be played, but this is far from saying that politics is the sole factor governing these decisions. On the contrary, the notion that "all is politics," implying that ability and rationality do not count, is the favorite dodge of incompetent persons.

Organizational politics in the ultimate sense is a phrase denoting those types of interpersonal behaviors by which managers relate to others while advancing themselves and, at the same time, advancing the welfare of the organization. Clearly, interpersonal relationships are only in part subject to deliberate calculation or manipulation. Preferences, trust, confidence, respect, and fun are undoubtedly more important to enduring human interrelationships.

There is a large element of spontaneity in interpersonal rela
tionships. However, strategic values are always present and are
inherent, since the parties to an interrelationship presumably
continue in it through perceiving, either consciously or unconsciously, that the gains exceed the costs. A coalition or a conspir-
acy assembled for a particular purpose is probably the most calculating of the possible interrelationship categories. But coalitions and conspiracies fade when their purposes are achieved or
when they are broken up by defensive maneuvers or by some
attacking element of the organization.

The term politics is often used to describe the behavior of
those persons in organizations who are skilled in advancing their
own cause, and in "playing the power game." Such criticisms are
often mingled with envy among the less politically adroit. Politicians seem to be the manipulators, the maneuverers, who are
good at protecting their own flanks. They hide their deficiencies
from those who count in the power game, put forward their best
front when it counts the most, and forge alliances with powerful
people who can bring them along in the organization with their
own advancement. Many harbor suspicions of the politically successful individual as a person not really competent technically or
substantively. To the politicians, appearance becomes more important than substance. To win, politicians must sell themselves
to the organization and to key individuals regardless of true
abilities.

Political behavior is more than a person-to-person struggle; it
involves the pitting of one domain against other domains. As a
group phenomenon much is at stake; much can be lost or much
can be gained. In large-scale political maneuvers, individual
managers may go unnoticed when their political behavior is subtle. The best politicians tend not to appear like politicians at all,
and if they can remain submerged in a group of allies, such as a
clique or a coalition, so much the better.

Furthermore, no executive can be political all of the time. One
has to choose carefully the times to become involved in a particular situation. Timing is important because political opportunities
tend to arise suddenly and not last for very long. Managers must
therefore seize the right moment. Politicians do not want to
waste their energies on the unimportant or the trivial nor take

too big a risk and make a mistake that will end their careers with the organization.

It is important for the politician-manager to give careful thought to friendships and loyalties in the organization and to the groups and individuals with which alliances are formed. He cannot afford to choose the wrong side. Yet the manager does not want to be a conformist, slavishly kowtowing to those who can do him some good.

In sum, the interrelationships among managers are not strictly interpersonal. Individual managers are representatives of their respective domains in transactions with outside groups or individuals. Effective domain management is needed to control transactions across boundaries, to establish group identities, and to engender loyalties and feelings of security on the part of organization members. The existence of boundary management problems adds a political dimension to the manager's tasks.

CHAPTER
5

Working with
Your Boss

As a manager, you are an important link in a complex web of personal and official relationships. Your domain of responsibilities can be maintained only through a satisfactory linkage to the rest of the organization.

The official relationships are reflected in the formal patterns of organization structure. They are revealed by charts, manuals, written delegations of authority, and established channels of communication. Your personal skills and strategies and those of others with whom you work determine the way in which these formal structures operate in daily practice on the job.

Your basic linkage to the rest of the system is through the mechanism of the hierarchy. The hierarchy represents a distribution of tasks and responsibilities by levels of authority. It is maintained by a reporting system in which the manager of each domain is connected to a higher level of authority under the supervision of a manager who directs the work of several related domains. In short, you have one or more bosses who are "above" you in the organization structure.

Most managers give very special attention to the nature of their relationships to their bosses. There are three reasons why you should consider this matter. First, your effectiveness as a manager is closely related to your ability to relate successfully to your boss. Second, your boss has great influence on the progress of your career. Your destiny in the organization is largely under his control. Third, you can learn a lot from him.

Let us first consider some of the conditions the hierarchy creates for you and your work. Then we will analyze a number of important aspects of your relationships to the boss.

The Hierarchy

Some organizations develop strong hierarchies, stressing authority, delegations, and clear-cut domains. Others employ a more loosely structured set of interrelationships among jobs and people which de-emphasizes internal boundaries and rigid, monolithic relationships. In either case, there is always a structure. Whether the hierarchy is formally composed of jobs, delegated authority, and assigned responsibility with people fitted to the structure, or whether people develop in their work the formal and informal apparatus they need, structure remains a fundamental element of all organizational processes. In a highly bureaucratic organization, tasks and positions predominate; in a looser, more flexible organization, hierarchies develop between groups, task forces, project teams, and resource persons of many types, including administrators who plan, assist, coordinate, and evaluate activities.

Even in the strongest hierarchy there are flexibilities and informalities. However, in such organizations informality may be regarded as a deviation to be minimized and controlled, and flexibility may be an accidental, unique occurrence. The danger is that the hierarchy may become an end in itself, rather than a means to given ends. The important thing is to design an organization structure most appropriate for the purposes to be served. An advertising agency might well utilize a high degree of informality whereas a military unit may require a high degree of structure and control.

To the hierarchy we can attribute much that accounts for the success of organizations and of individuals within them. For one thing, it provides a measure—albeit a rough one—of a manager's success. But success in climbing the hierarchy is not always equivalent to or commensurate with the achievement of useful, desirable goals.

A manager who wishes to advance his career needs a set of social and political skills fully as much as experience, know-how, and technical skills. If the hierarchy is not overemphasized, the creative manager can avoid excessive concentration on self-aggrandizement and intense competition with peers. This strategy accepts the reality of the hierarchy but permits the manager to focus on positive accomplishment. Backbiting, talebearing, rumormongering, playing for the record, and back scratching can give way to the honest expressions of ideas, the logics of the tasks to be performed, and more open communication.

A second attribute of the hierarchical structuring of organizations is that it provides logical, systematic categories or domains of task behavior; the framework for duties and responsibilities; and role prescriptions that produce purposeful, predictable behavior. The structure reveals formal relationships that condition the expectations others hold toward your work and releases some behaviors while it constrains others to predictable limits. A large proportion of the organization's effort is fitted to activities that can be routinized. Nonroutine activities are not necessarily precluded, but they can be observed and monitored at appropriate times and places at various points in the hierarchy.

The hierarchy is thus a rational-logical tool, highly useful when held in check and implemented with creative intelligence. The failures and faults ascribed to bureaucracies with strong hierarchies are not necessarily inherent in the nature of this tool. They are the consequences of the failure to understand hierarchy as a means to given desirable ends and of the failure of managers to acquire and utilize its positive attributes.

How can creative managers derive the best results from hierarchical arrangements? First, they can accept the fact that some hierarchy is necessary to all organized endeavor. Second, they can recognize that no given hierarchy is a permanent or a perfect answer to the needs an organization is designed to fulfill. Third, they can recognize that for all its vaunted rigidity, the hierarchy has its flexibilities which the judicious manager can comprehend. Hierarchical elements do change, and in fact must change as needs and objectives change. Fourth, they can learn to avoid blind subservience, loyalty, and obedience to form while substance is ignored. The unquestioning, fawning "yes-man" is the very opposite of the creative manager even within a hierarchical system.

Creative managers know when to fight and when to bend to the will of the hierarchy. They learn to take their responsibilities seriously but not the fluff and fog of ceremony and protocol. Active, open, and constructive resistance to artificial or imagined pressures or to undue constraints is preferable to martyred acceptance of the status quo. There is no such thing as a competent manager who enjoys a risk-free compatability with the hierarchy.

The dynamics of the hierarchy are often hidden from view, masked by strange protocols, which are cultivated by status systems, and by the defense mechanisms of mystic domains. The creative manager himself needs defense mechanisms that help him maintain his composure and his *savoir-faire* in the face of hierarchical barriers to accomplishment.

The necessary mechanisms are not those designed for self-protection or aggrandizement. The creative manager is not afraid to take risks, to make courageous and timely decisions, and to capitalize on flexibilities available to him in carrying out missions. By utilizing key defense mechanisms, the creative manager minimizes fear, anxiety, and me-tooism.

Among the most useful defense mechanisms are (1) the use of firm deadlines for yourself and for your subordinates; (2) careful control of the way you use your time, especially discretionary or free time, and of the way you let others use your time; (3) effective planning that anticipates the consequences of decisions and actions; and (4) care in the acceptance of tasks and responsibilities to make sure you concentrate on what you can do best.

Many organizations are trying to de-emphasize the facets of hierarchy that obstruct creativity, create false or divisive goals, and reduce the individual to dependency and conformity. Even though you are working for an organization that has not gone as far in this direction as you might prefer, you can do much to run your own part of the organization in such a way as to loosen the awkward, irrelevant, and restrictive hold of the bureaucracy over individuals.

The first step is to set an example. Examine your own management style to see whether you are geared to tight hierarchical principles. If so, ask yourself where you can ease up without creating undue discord. Any changes in your management style should be gradual and undertaken only after careful analysis.

You've gotten help from management training programs and from reading books. You can get further help from the same sources and from colleagues you respect.

If you are depending unduly on structure, positional authority, rules, regulations, and the protocols of formal organizations, you may not be relying enough on leadership skill, logical analysis, technical know-how, persuasion, and teamwork.

Relating to Your Boss

You are both a manager and an employee. Your role as an employee can be as carefully designed as your role as a manager.

The role of the subordinate is a difficult one. Trained to give orders rather than take them, your understanding of the requirements of this role is largely intuitive. Organizations have programs to develop in executives the skills of command, direction, and leadership, but not subordination. Moreover your acts of leadership, command, and direction seem more natural, more comfortable than the role expected of the subordinate. In directing others, your self-interest, your ego, or your favorite aspirations are less at stake. Your downward communications can be, and often are, relatively impersonal in the sense that the authority inherent in your position can support your personal leadership in getting subordinates to do your bidding. The bureaucratic system may support you in managing subordinates, but it affords you few sustaining props in *being* a subordinate.

A certain ambivalence thus comes to characterize most managers. A manager may feel strong and secure in his position and at the same time have anxieties about his own status as an employee. Just as he desires subordinates to obey and to mold themselves to the image he prescribes, he is also aware that the same demands are being made on him.

When the ambivalence shows, the manager displeases both boss and subordinates, because the two roles become ambiguous. Therefore the manager needs to develop a rationale for the performance of these two roles, reducing wherever possible their inconsistencies and incompatabilities.

The first step in achieving a more workable harmony in the two roles is to recognize them both for what they are. They are both necessary. No manager escapes their hold. Successful managers use the existence of the two roles to further their own development.

Your experiences in the two roles can be usefully contrasted and compared. As a boss, you get reactions from subordinates. As a subordinate, you experience direction and influence from above. It is up to you to evaluate their general impact upon yourself.

The classic concept of the manager caught "in the middle" of organizational pressures has been related in the past mainly to first-line supervisors. But it is clear that nearly every manager is "in the middle," that is, a linking-pin in the hierarchical system of levels. The significance of this linking position is that it connects work teams as well as individuals.*

The Upward Focus

By concentrating on the upward direction of influence and communication, you can learn much of value in developing your leadership skills. But more is meant than merely imitating the habits and ideas originating further up. It is natural, of course, that you may acquire certain stylistic elements of leadership from a superior, particularly one you admire. Both good and bad habits may consciously or unconsciously be observed and imitated. Emulation of your superior may even be part of a grand strategy of flattering the boss. Payoffs of many kinds may ensue from these forms of imitation, although the price of attaining them in terms of accompanying or subsequent consequences must always be weighed. Nevertheless, a top-flight manager will go far beyond the level of mere imitation. The creative manager needs to elicit from above as many ideas as possible that favor the growth of knowledge and the increase of opportunities to practice higher management skills.

Thus, what you need is a keenly analytical approach not only to your boss's behavior but to your own and to the characteristics of

*See Rensis Likert, *New Patterns of Management* (New York: McGraw-Hill, 1961).

the man-boss relationships in which you are involved. The ana
lytical approach is a cautious one. It does not take things at their
face value. By going beneath the surface to a deeper analytical
level, you can develop the true significance of various observed
phenomena. Judgments, however, must be limited to those
which facts and events support. Indeed, judgments reached too
quickly are the enemy of analytical precision.

To illustrate the above points, consider the problems of the
manager whose boss has communicated very little specific information about what duties and responsibilties are expected of
him. This is a general characteristic of many bosses; they assume
that the behavior they expect is obvious. They are content to
accept a standard role performance as perceived and carried out
by experienced managers. In such a situation, a manager has to
decide whether or not to accept a superior's willingness to let
him structure an appropriate role. This decision depends on siz-
ing up both the higher manager and himself, for within the total
behavior pattern of each lies the key to working out an effective,
long-run relationship. Creative managers need to discover why
their bosses do not carefully structure their roles. Sometimes it is
because the boss has complete confidence and trust in the subordinate's abilities. Often, however, the laissez-faire attitude of a
superior is rooted in a captious, more freakish desire to give the
subordinate a chance to flounder and fail. The free hand allowed
the subordinate can in truth be a snare used by a boss to criticize
or to punish the subordinate for mistakes.

The manager under these conditions needs a strategy to offset
the risks entailed in the "free hand" philosophy which might
otherwise be enjoyed. But the strategy to be developed, and the
means by which it is to be evolved and applied, are dependent on
the other half of the relationship: the manager's own temperament, makeup, skills, insights, and abilities. The manager must
first correctly judge the motives, attitudes, and behavior of the
superior. Beyond this, the creative manager needs to ask what
kind of a relationship is best. The next step is to measure the
discrepancy between what is and what should be, Developing
strategy is then a matter of estimating the costs and consequences of the contemplated actions. Thus one might decide that
it is necessary to force the superior to acknowledge his respon-

sibilities. Creative managers know when to insist on a clarification of the nature and scope of their responsibilities.

Another approach to the above set of problems that would avoid drafting an all-inclusive set of understandings is for the manager to examine each task, project, or assignment on an *ad hoc* basis to see whether it is possible to avoid pitfalls by advance planning. Suppose further that the manager knows nothing of the technical requirements of a task and has never had any experience in this area. There are two ready alternatives: (1) to ask the boss to get someone else to do it and admit deficiencies or (2) to plow through the assignment without question hoping that deficiencies will stay hidden. But a third possibility may be to negotiate with the superior to head off future criticisms and trouble. This alternative involves admitting one's limitations or lack of technical skills and undertaking the assignment as a challenge. Such a strategy requires full resources, including adequate outside consultants, and the superior's help along the way.

Here some will object to the idea of a subordinate structuring the decision behavior of a superior. But this is precisely what differentiates the creative from the inept manager. The skillful manager knows what tasks require in terms of resources and technical knowledge and that it is foolhardy to undertake a major responsibility under any conditions other than those which will assure its success. Negotiating for maximum conditions favoring successful performance of the assigned tasks makes sense. Presumably both the superior and the subordinate want results. At the very least, the manager puts on record the need for realistically viewing the conditions that affect results. Once attention has been drawn to the possible difficulties, the manager can proceed to carry out the tasks in greater confidence.

In the best of all worlds, we thrive on clarity and correctness of delegated responsibilities. That this ideal is seldom achieved among managers gives rise to the need for negotiation and the acceptance of some ambiguities. For example, people every day do the following things:

Have more than one boss.
Have responsibility without authority.
Assume authority and responsibilities they have not been assigned.

Change their duties, tasks, and responsibilities without per-
mission or without clearing with bosses, subordinates, or
peers.
Accept an inequality between authority and responsibility.

Acceptance and Rejection

Knowing when to be accepting toward higher authority and
when to resist it is one of the arts of creative management. This
means that the manager realizes that there are degrees of acceptance and degrees of resistance. It also means that the manager confronts daily decisions as to how much acceptance or how
much resistance to direct toward others in the organization.

Stable, orderly conditions of work cannot exist without a reasonable amount of acceptance of higher authority by the members of an organization. This acceptance is a kind of self-discipline
by which managers submerge their individual autonomy to the
extent necessary for the effective pursuit of common endeavors.
The creative manager learns to relate to superiors with appropriate acceptance without indulging in slavish conformity or
cringing subservience. This requires him to accept the responsibility of conveying differing judgments, opinions, or beliefs and
the reasons behind them. It also requires resisting the tempta-
tion to preserve personal security by arranging matters so that
the boss alone gets whacked when something goes wrong.

Avoidance of confrontation over significant issues and ignoring
potential power struggles is a form of administrative cowardice,
showing that the individual does not really care enough about the
organization to defend his position in the world of action. A
manager can carry on quite well even though he loses a few
confrontations over a period of time. However, if the confrontations are frequent and the loss rate high, the manager has
grounds for considering whether the job or the organization is
appropriate. One who is simply not on the right wavelength with
the boss or with fellow workers may need to plan a change of
jobs.

You know you are in the right organization and in the right job
if you feel free to express yourself and to make your contribution
without retribution or recrimination from those above you. The

organization or the boss that exacts unquestioned obedience and constant subservience is not worth caring about, for respect and acceptance are lacking for both leaders and followers.

The greater the degree to which your position is structured, routinized, regimented, or fortified by rules, regulations, habit, and precedents, the less is your flexibility and potential for innovation and creativity. But the higher you go in your organization, the less structured will your tasks and responsibilities become. Interpersonal relationships begin to count for more than specific task performance as such. The higher you go, the more demanding your work will be and the less secure you are likely to feel in it. Accordingly, you will seek to justify your boss's confidence in your independence, autonomy, and flexibility. Specific results and a successful track record in your work will cause your boss to believe in you.

Even though yours is a world of highly concentrated, well focused effort, you must devote your attention to two elements simultaneously: the cultivation of the relationships and the creditable achievement of goals. If your needs for clarity of job definition, task responsibilities, and performance criteria are too strong you may be destined not to rise above middle management levels in your organization. Rising to positions of greater responsibility is not for everyone. If, however, you aspire to higher goals, you can count on some hard challenges and greater demands upon your mental and physical energies.

People have certain needs which cause them to be relatively dependent on bosses and organizations. These needs are stronger for some than others. Therefore it is important to know yourself. However, dependence upon an autocratic supervisor is one of the escape hatches that people use to avoid shouldering responsibility themselves. If your boss issues orders and makes all the major decisions, he, rather than you, becomes the scapegoat if anything should go wrong.

Within your specific field of effort and enterprise, you can become quite self-confident and assured. It is when you are persuaded to go beyond these boundaries that you may experience anxiety and difficulty. One trouble with excessive dependence upon a boss or anyone else is that a crisis or a serious challenge can throw you off your pace. It may lead you to break down in the face of the unfamiliar, the new and different. It may cause you to resist change and to take extreme measures to hold your domain together. Since overdependence leads to indecision, worry, and post-decision anxiety and since it exaggerates preexisting tendencies by the boss to be rigid and bureaucratic, overdependency can be costly to the organization. It may produce low morale and cost you the respect of your group. It leads to "going-by-the-book," conformity, and blind adherence to established precedents, rules, and procedures. In these circumstances, your learning and growth are inhibited. The new, the innovative, or the untried is avoided rather than grappled with. Personal conflict arises in the form of sidetracking or eliminating potentially threatening subordinates.

Robert McMurry, a noted industrial psychologist, has listed the following patterns which characterize overdependence:

1. Resistance to change, a tendency to live in the past.
2. Acute indecisiveness, a reluctance to give a "yes" or "no" answer to any question.
3. Abdication of supervisory responsibilities, that is, overpermissiveness.
4. Absolute autocracy or blind "going by the book."
5. A tendency to play favorites or have strong negative or positive biases.
6. A reluctance to take responsibility for mistakes and errors, being a "buck passer" or the "alibi artist."
7. An incapacity to learn from one's mistakes.
8. Extreme defensiveness when criticized.
9. Disorganization and panic when under prolonged or heavy pressure, the desire to flee or withdraw.
10. An intolerance for strong, competent subordinates.
11. A reluctance to follow through on difficult or threatening assignments.
12. The manifestation of hostility and chronic dissatisfaction.
13. Inability to delegate.
14. Over-preoccupation with detail.
15. A tendency to "lean" on superiors for guidance and help.*

*Robert N. McMurry, "Management's Achilles' Heel: Overdependence," *Michigan Business Review*, November 1973, pp. 14-24.

Practical Considerations

Your boss has a great influence over what you can become. People shape people. They are, to a large extent, what others, especially authority figures, help them to become. You are what others help you to be, and you help others to be what they are. This is the core of the interpersonal theory of personality pioneered in social psychiatry by Harry Stack Sullivan.* He believes that an individual is shaped chiefly by the nature of his relationships with others at home, social events, and at work. This influence begins at birth, continues throughout life, and includes not only actual dealings with others but fantasized relationships as well, both in waking and sleeping dreams, memories, and in hallucinations.

If interactions with your boss are rewarding for you, your personality will tend to develop favorably. If they are upsetting, your personality may become disturbed or distorted. Sullivan believes that fear of social disapproval has a greater impact than some of the influences identified by Freud, such as tensions arising from unsatisfied physical needs.

As a creative manager you can do many things to strengthen the formal and informal relations with your boss. By carefully studying the boss you can know his strengths and weaknesses. Become analytical and shrewdly observant. Don't take things for granted—either the substance of how you stand with the boss or what the boss thinks and feels. To avoid reliance on speculation, learn to use the devices of probing, questioning, and observing to gather as factual a basis as possible for your conclusions.

Another technique is to use specific suggestions. Sometimes a manager holds back through fear, imagined or real. When the time is right, a well-placed suggestion can do you and the organization a lot of good. How long has it been since you made a specific, helpful suggestion to your boss? You have to let your boss know what you expect, just as the boss will no doubt let you know what he expects of you. Unfortunately, candid and accurate intercommunication between bosses and subordinates is seldom attained. But you can more readily take the initiative in clearing

---

*Harry Stack Sullivan, *Concepts of Modern Psychiatry* (New York: W. W. Norton, Inc., 1947).

things up with your boss. If questions arise, take them up with the boss.

Some individuals are highly suggestive, meaning that they are almost always ready to follow a positive suggestion strongly put forth. If you discover that your boss fits into this category, you will have to use this concept with great caution. It cannot be used often or without careful thought. With such a boss, you can often be very positive in rejecting his ideas or suggestions, thus successfully reversing a decision you don't like. But it is wise to do this only if the matter is of extreme importance to you or to your part of the organization.

Another important creative function you can serve as a manager is to interpret to your boss the feelings and attitudes of your own subordinates. You are truly in the middle here, and the position is a difficult one to be in. The following guidelines apply in this situation:

- ☐ Be sure that you are actually aware of the feelings and attitudes within your group before you try to transmit them upward.
- ☐ Guard against distortions, exaggerations, and biases of your own by which you may be tempted to embellish your reporting upward.
- ☐ Be wary of exaggerating the strength and nature of what you are reporting upward. Don't try for more power or effect than you need to accomplish your purpose; in other words, avoid overkill.

At some time, you may find yourself in the position of working for a boss who is younger than you are, and less experienced. This happens when organizations use a "fast track" system for advancing able "young turks." It happens wherever an organization evaluates potential abilities and contributions more highly than past experience in the organization.

To meet this situation, it helps to understand the basic characteristics of such a boss. The young person who has been promoted over the heads of older, more experienced persons is often impatient. Anxieties that stem from his lack of experience and maturity will develop. Willingness to accept failure or mistakes on the part of others may be absent. Such a boss may also be extremely self-critical and excessively concerned over both his and others' mistakes.

You will be tempted to help such a boss, because having a successful superior will advance your own interests. But younger bosses are disinclined to accept advice gracefully. You can't count on their overt appreciation for your help. Therefore you may have to help without getting specific credit for doing so.

The young manager for whom you work is under extra pressures to make good, working very hard to build a record of achievement. This may lead to his putting immediate, short-range goals above long-term interests. Your guidance here may be very helpful.

As the older subordinate of a younger boss, you may be tempted to test your superior by not helping or by putting up roadblocks. This strategy is probably self-defeating in the long run since the superior will ultimately be aware of your actions. The boss who succeeds in spite of your handicaps will look very good indeed. If the boss fails, you may look as bad as he does. At the same time, it is possible that you and others may push and prod well enough to bring forth the best work from the total group.

Realizing that the younger boss is in a difficult position is helpful. Up to a point, you may wish to pull occasional chestnuts out of the fire for your boss. But if the need for rescue is continuous, you are likely to lose respect for your boss.

Being the son of a boss (S.O.B.) has problems similar to those of having an older boss, with additional complications. If your father is your immediate boss, or even if he is several levels above you, you face the specter of alleged favoritism. Even if the allegation is unjustified, it can hinder your relationships with others. Others will feel threatened by you, believing you are after their jobs.

Often a parent will go out of his way to make a son or daughter employee earn his way. Moreover, a parent may feel threatened by the advancement of his child and thus hold him or her back "to gain experience, seasoning, and maturity."

Jennings has written that the manager most likely to succeed is the one who (1) rescues the boss from his mistakes, (2) maintains the authority delegated, (3) is satisfied with the role of subordinate, (4) projects the image of the boss that the boss desires, and (5) engages in predictable behavior.* These precepts, however, are governed by a number of assumptions concerning the way bureaucratic organizations operate. Offsetting them are the manager's needs for fulfillment, meaningful work, independence, autonomy, and individuality. Every man-boss relationship ultimately represents a resolution of the pressures for conformity and the pressure for autonomy.

*Eugene E. Jennings, "How to Satisfy the Boss," *Nation's Business*, October 1971, pp. 14-47.

CHAPTER
6

Building an Effective Work Group

What is so different about being a manager? One very good answer to this question is that managers are responsible for results that other people help them achieve, results that they cannot accomplish through their own efforts alone.

As a manager you are dependent in part upon your superior and on colleagues outside your immediate domain. To a far greater extent than most managers recognize, you are dependent upon your subordinates. They have the power, if they so desire, to make you or break you.

Your dependence on others contrasts sharply with the image of autonomy, independence, and aggressive decision making that also pervades your work. But in modern, complex organizations seldom are significant accomplishments wholly the product of one person's effort.

Dependency relationships are always two-way streets. There is a mutuality of interests between you and your boss and between you and your subordinates. There will always be give and take, honest differences of opinion, and even outright conflict. Success hinges on a balance in favor of the recognition of mutual interests that transcend deep, unresolved conflict.

The manager's primary task is to use personal energies and organizational resources to achieve the desired results effectively. This goes beyond the fair and intelligent allocation of economic resources and development of good human relations

with subordinates, to include the effective leadership and direction of the work group as a whole. Organizations are to a large
extent service minded; they generally have a strong orientation
toward consumer or client satisfaction as a primary goal. Failure
to operate the organization as an effective work team will most
certainly be reflected in undesirable effects at the point of cus-
tomer contact.

Importance of the Team

Building an effective working team is one of a manager's responsibilities. This team will consist of other managers subordinate to
you, plus technicians, clerical staff, and other kinds of workers.
The basis for your team is the entire unit, not merely the managers. Everyone deserves to be on the team, and undue separation between managers and others in your group will serve to
discourage an integration of interests and efforts.

It is important for you to arrive at a personal commitment to
the idea of team building if it is to be successful. This will take
substantial, patient, and continuous effort on your part and will
test your capability for bringing out the best in individuals whose
talents vary widely.

At the outset you must decide to pay more than lip service to
the concept by reviewing the strengths and weaknesses of your
own leadership behavior. A consummate degree of courage and
integrity is required to acknowledge one's own drawbacks. However, if drawbacks do exist, they are at least partly apparent to
subordinates and colleagues. Facing them squarely will earn you
some "brownie" points for frankness and pave the way for enlisting the cooperation of the group's members in the team's objectives.

To review your own leadership style, you must observe the
behavior of subordinates and colleagues, for their attitudes and
actions will reflect how well you have been doing. You can search
for clues that indicate a different point of view from your own
concerning how the group is doing.

Your concerns should also include making those above you in
the organization aware of your group. To do this you should be
sure to report to the chief executive the progress, accom-

plishments, and specific examples of success of the team to justify its continuance and to win further support. You should also take pains to hide, rationalize, or eliminate the unsolved problems or nasty difficulties that pervade most groups. These two behavior characteristics—publicizing the positive and concealing the negative—are natural constructs of your managerial role. In behaving this way, you are meeting some of the expectations of superiors, subordinates, and colleagues. You simply do not and cannot tell all you know, because you recognize obligations to protect and strengthen your subordinates, to obtain adequate resources for them, and to help them use these resources wisely. You also know that you are accountable to higher management for the actions and results of the group.

The above two thought patterns may frequently cause you to develop blind spots in viewing the activities of subordinates and colleagues, accounting for discrepancies between your view and theirs about what is going on. Nevertheless, cues and signals come out of the interactions and activities of group managers that you should take account of in guiding the work of the group.

Building a strong work team thus presents you with the need to critically assess your habits, motives, and management style and, in addition, to examine the raw material out of which the work team may be built. Putting the idea over on more than a lip-service basis leads to the most difficult part of the whole process: recognizing that you, yourself, may need to change and that you have changes to bring about within the group. Most vital of all, however, is the fact that these changes will increase the importance of the overt roles you, yourself, play. Members of the group must be allowed greater latitude of action, upward communication, and decision making. They have to be trusted, and you will often have to assume the risks of their mistakes and failures. Your leadership style may tend to undergo a change from the direct use of comfortable authority inherent in your position. Your work may come to consist of a more indirect but highly planned effort to employ the subtleties of influence rather than the crunch of power and authority.

Although we are likely to judge ourselves by our intentions, we tend to judge others by their actions. In building a team, managers have to explain their actions and understand the intentions of others. This is difficult because it goes against the grain of action-oriented managerial philosophies.

Explaining your actions to the members of your team helps to train and educate them beyond their routine duties. It helps them to fit their work more closely to yours. It gives them a frame of reference—a set of guidelines that provides a model for shaping their intentions.

Understanding the intentions of team members improves your analysis of their needs, aspirations, and consequent behavior. It tells you the "why or why not" of their actions, provides you with a more complete view of each team member as a person, and permits you to make more accurate comparisons of members of the team. It gives you the basis for fitting their work together. When intentions are separate from team objectives, you can take preventive action to relate team members to each other.

There is the possibility that team building may be difficult due to technological or structural factors. Technological factors are frequently important in determining the various groups and sub-groups in an organization. For example, it is probably easier to develop team spirit when technology permits all members of the group to be present and to interact with one another than when the members are geographically separated, as in the case of a field sales force. Another example is found in cases where sub-groups form around technological requirements so diverse as to preclude building the groups into a team because all the members do not develop a common framework of discourse within which they can evolve common views and experiences. In most organizations, however, there would appear to be little inherent difficulty in building better teamwork.

Selecting Team Members

Building a team right from the start is a rare opportunity that comes infrequently for most managers. The advantage lies in starting afresh, selecting people for their special interests and capabilities. Motivation is high because challenges and opportunities abound. People can create the organization and its work rather than fit themselves to already existing structures, tasks, or rules of the game.

More typically, managers must work with an already existing group. Unless the managers are expected to play a "hatchet man" role, there is a tendency to accept current members of the group. A vital first step is to appraise the strengths and weaknesses of individuals and to analyze the degree of team-mindedness already present.

Thus there are two main ways by which you can proceed to build a strong team. You can move on both at once because they are compatible with each other. First, you build your team by carefully selecting its members. Second, you work with the individuals and the group to bring about learning, motivated behavior, smooth coordination, and effective task performance through team efforts.

The first activity expresses the need not only to recruit and hire good people but to choose people for a particular purpose—a purpose the manager has made plans for in advance so that the selection advances the team's total capacities as much as possible. The latter activity acknowledges the fact that newly employed persons seldom fit a work group perfectly; candidates for employment do not match the ideal standards set up in the position qualifications.

You cannot build your work team solely by finding the right people and hiring them. But the individuals you hire represent commitments that you may have to live with for quite some time. As a result, you need to make the best selections you can, given the limitations of cost and time. Every position vacancy is an opportunity to build and rebuild your group. It is possible that you will make a mistake in judging applicants, but you should never knowingly settle for less than the best with respect to your group's needs. You need persons whose abilities and personal characteristics are commensurate with the needs of the developing team.

An excellent procedure for filling existing vacancies from a team point of view is first to consider the task structure. Is it still appropriate and will it continue to be? Can existing team members absorb all or part of the tasks? Should there be a rearrangement of existing responsibilities before applicants are considered?

A second step is to tap the resources of the existing team

members to determine their suggestions and preferences. They can provide insights and suggestions for revising the task structure and for recruiting potential applicants. It is often desirable to give team members a voice in the ultimate selection of a new member.

Building the Team

Let us consider in detail the problems of building a strong and effective work team from your present group. This presumes that the component members are inclined to remain in the organization for relatively long periods of time. The organization tends to be relatively stable but some changes will occur. The vacancies that do occur can be utilized as opportunities to further strengthen the team, but the more critical problem is to deal successfully with the existing group as a whole so that its available energies are directed toward suitable goals.

Five managerial problem areas will greatly affect your success in building a strong working team: motivation, communication, adjudication, evaluation, and informal groups.

MOTIVATION

Like love of country, everyone agrees that motivation is important. It reflects the zeal, enthusiasm, and propelling force behind the efforts of an individual or a group. To know the motive behind an action is to know the reasons why the observed behavior is what it is.

If you have attended training courses on "managerial motivation," you have probably been asked to believe that you and only you are responsible for motivating subordinates to extraordinary feats of productivity, loyalty, and service. This is only partly true. Certainly you play a significant role in the daily scenes of action. As a manager and a leader, you face problems of motivation every day. Motivating individuals and groups is a fundamental part of any problem you tackle. But there is more to it than merely the art of getting others to do as you want them to do.

Motivation is an extremely complex subject. No one can hand you a list of things to do that guarantees the motivation of others. A first step, and a very important one, is to ask yourself what motivates you? Why are you doing what you are doing? Why do you care? What do you care most about? What are you trying to get out of the system? What are you trying to give to the system? Knowing something about your own motives yields insights for understanding the motivations of others. The motivating forces that direct your subordinates are often the same ones that influence you.

Motivation may be regarded as an inner state of human beings. It consists of needs and drives which direct goal-seeking energies and ambitions. Thus you cannot really "motivate" another person. What you can do is understand the way conditions you control or influence may affect the behavior of that person. Then you can work on the conditions to bring about the constructive, improved behavior that you desire in those around you.

Motivation is a challenge to every manager not only because of its complexity but also because each individual is unique. Moreover, motivation does not exist at a constant level; it changes as people and their situations change. Successful motivation depends on knowing each subordinate well enough to take into account his variations from ordinary patterns.

It is apparent that in most organizations more than half the capabilities of most people go untapped because the conditions of motivation have been neglected. Indeed, R. Buckminster Fuller has argued that, in many cases, individuals get de-motivated much of the time. He has expressed the opinion that all of humanity is born with more gifts than we know and the hypothesis that most babies are born geniuses and just get de-geniused rapidly: "Unfavorable circumstances, shortsightedness, frayed nervous systems, ignorantly articulated love, and fear of elders tend to shut off many of the child's brain capability waves."*

Motivation concerns the mainsprings by which people are activated to do what they do. It is the key to understanding and directing others. Management literature is chock full of advice about human needs, motives, and drives. You should study this literature with the objective of applying it to the team situation, because motivating individuals is one thing and motivating indi-

---

*R. Buckminster Fuller, *Utopia or Oblivion: The Prospects for Humanity* (New York: Bantam Books, Inc., 1969), p. 10.

viduals as members of a work team is quite another. Motivation is a complex process requiring the utmost finesse. Research to date indicates the following general guidelines:

☐ Money is not a primary motivating force in situations where pay scales are fairly adjusted among members of a group and where levels of pay are fitted to community wage scales.

☐ Conversely, monetary rewards can evoke adverse feelings if inequities in the group or with external wage scales become apparent.

☐ Judging what motivates a particular person at a particular time is a complex act of interpretation based on overt actions or stated attitudes, which puts the manager in danger of being wrong in judgments about motivation.

☐ People are to a large extent motivated by conditions and events *outside* the organization as well as inside. The manager who attempts to set up in the work team the most favorable motivating conditions may still not succeed in motivating peak performance among work team members unless both inside and outside factors are considered. Also, with poor motivation inside, group members may still perform well, but obtain their inner-life satisfactions externally.

☐ In the work team, motivation becomes everyone's responsibility—not merely the manager's. This does not result in less work for the manager, however, since the efforts of team members to achieve better results may build up strains and tensions with which the manager will have to deal.

COMMUNICATION

Communication problems mount in building a strong work team. Everyone in the group develops an intense desire to be communicated with; breaches in the communication pipelines become more serious because they affect more people and can seriously affect the group result. The manager, therefore, faces the problems not only of communicating to his group members but also of getting them to communicate properly with one another and with him.

Physical work arrangements play an important part in the communication process. Thus the manager can profitably review the work flow, technical procedures and policies, and work situations. This review should consider the objective of building the team. In most cases, such a review results in a less rigid and more flexible movement of persons within the work environment. If the group is allowed to work out its own physical arrangements, greater flexibility usually results and communication is enhanced.

The central fact to be communicated and re-communicated to a work team is the mission of the group as a whole. This must be a meaningful mission and one capable of enlisting the sympathies and energies of all members of the group. The mission must fit the facts or at least not appear to contradict the facts as they are known to group members. There is room for conflict and disagreement here, since managers often pose the mission in its most idealistic, advanced forms. Those occupied with the struggle to carry out the mission often react by becoming discouraged or antagonistic. Too general a mission is hard to sell; too detailed a mission can generate specific objections. The manager needs to find a point of balance between these two extremes.

ADJUDICATION

The third major problem in building a work team is adjudication. Adjudication is that aspect of the manager's role in which he makes decisions to resolve issues between persons. For example, if two file clerks ask for the same day off and the office is very busy, the manager decides that only one can be spared. The manager usually searches for facts that will help decide which request to grant. To do this he questions the clerks to probe the reasons for their requests and weighs all the relevant factors. The relative merits of the two cases are thus used to decide the issue.

The adjudication process is a problem because the manager's decision usually favors one person and disfavors another. Moreover, problems of adjudication are usually urgent, with both contenders eager for a quick decision. Some managers postpone decisions in the usually futile hope that the problem and the decision required will disappear, but promptness works to the advantage of the manager. Fairness is a desirable attribute of adjudication decisions, but a synthetic or spurious fairness is not a good substitute for the *right* decision. For example, fairness in assigning duties to six subordinates might superficially at least indicate that the available tasks should be divided equally among them. The six subordinates might feel that this would be fair. But if the abilities of the six particular persons vary markedly, it would not be right, from a performance point of view, to divide the tasks evenly.

Adjudication imputes a wisdom to managers which many feel they do not have. There is always the risk of being wrong. However, subordinates will usually tolerate an occasional error more readily than they will acquiesce to delay or temporizing on the settlement of issues among them.

In the adjudication process the manager finds that power varies widely among colleagues and subordinates; since the powerful may attempt to use their power to the disadvantage of the less powerful, the adjudicator finds himself confronting the most powerful in the group in order to protect the others. This is not fun, or even pleasant, and the manager needs to have positive power relationships with others higher up in order to deal effectively with the power centers in the group. If the powerful can bypass him and influence superiors in their own favor, the leader loses support that he needs to authenticate and legitimize decisions.

Thus building a work team requires coming to grips with coalitions and complex alignments within and without the group. Some managers dismiss these notions as mere "politics." The realistic ones are aware that work does not occur in a vacuum but only as a result of the combined efforts of people. Therefore, it is not a waste of time for the manager to attend to political questions within the organization. Rather it is an essential ingredient of effective action.

EVALUATION

Evaluation, the fourth problem area, has many characteristics similar to those of adjudication. Evaluation is as difficult for the manager as adjudication, and creates as many problems among subordinates—perhaps more. The core element in evaluation, as in adjudication, is the selection and clarification of the standards to be applied. The imperative of fairness, however subjective, remains crucial.

Evaluative opinions are rampant in all organizations. It is therefore a legitimate and necessary form of managerial action to systematize and control the evaluations that really count. Two forms of evaluation require the manager's attention: evaluation of the work team or group by himself, by its members, and by others in the organization, and evaluation of the individuals who make up the team.

The work team needs a strong identity as a group in its own right. The very formation of such a group causes others to judge its performance and its character, its image and its role relative to the organization as a whole. To say "we are a widget manufacturer" is also to call attention to the fact that there is an external environment, "non-widget manufacturing" possibilities. An organization's involvement with outsiders gives them the right to evaluate it on logical or nonlogical grounds.

Now the external image depends largely upon what the group and its members do. Therefore the manager's evaluations of internal activities are important, as are the evaluative feelings and attitudes of group members toward the manager, toward each other, and toward the group as a whole. In a more perfect world, the logic of all this would be compelling, and the manager would have no problems. But in most organizations, the interests and objectives of the individuals comprising a work group do not perfectly match the needs of the group itself or the organization as a whole. Some group members become nonconformists, threatening the group with liaisons outside it or with withdrawal or nonperformance of an essential part of the team's work. Talk of loyalty or teamwork in such cases has a hollow ring and tends to evoke resentment and further opposition.

The manager, seeking to maintain the group's team effectiveness, needs to communicate his evaluation of the group's progress as a group as well as of its overall performance. He also needs to face the intransigent and problem-creating people within the group and make clear his power to evaluate them on both the grounds of their contributions to the team and their personal productive efforts. Evaluation thus becomes an instrument of positive control as well as a potential motivation force.

When evaluating a group as a work team, the manager will perhaps be more objective, thus appearing to be more correct, than when evaluating the individual members. This is because the individual contributions and responsibilities are submerged and diffused among all group members. With individuals there is a greater emotional involvement and a personal stake in the matters about which their superior's judgments are given.

Whether the manager likes it or not, evaluation is inevitable. Some managers ignore or avoid this responsibility, but subordinates appear to seek definite guidelines so that they will know how others think they are doing. Even with careful effort to develop and use good standards, evaluation remains a judgmental process because standards cannot be precise enough to remove subjective elements.

INFORMAL GROUP RELATIONS

You will need to pursue your team-building effort in both the formal and informal spheres of organization behavior. Formal organization consists of specifying the task content of positions, delegation of authority, establishment of control mechanisms, and systemization of communication channels. Informal structures have been less clearly described. They are not deliberately created by managers. They arise out of the normal propensity of human beings to enlarge the meaning of their interaction with others in a group. The informal structure is basically superimposed over and interlocked with the formal structure.

Managers are often more concerned with the formal structure since its rational basis is more evident than that of the informal structure. However, both exist to meet a wide spectrum of needs which in fact are shared by both systems.

Some have suggested that the formal-informal dichotomy is unrealistic and is not meaningful in understanding organizations. But this argument is objectively specious, since the two types are clearly identifiable. They are both structural in character, and both serve as frameworks for actions and decisions.

Most managers distrust informal organization because they are unfamiliar with it. Some are fearful of its latent powers and distrust its legitimacy. What they fail to realize is the inevitability of informal relationships. Moreover, some skepticism derives from the reluctance to face interpersonal relationships, the fear of undue invasions of privacy, and the difficulties of understanding the complex, mysterious behavior of people. So much effort goes into working with the more familiar formal organization that there is often little time or inclination left to deal with the subtleties of the informal aspects of the group.

We are suggesting here that one cannot build an effective team on formal relationships alone. The very concept of a team implies the full set of characteristics and behaviors that apply to people at work. We are further suggesting that the manager ought to understand informal relationships, participate in them, and use them to strengthen his group efforts.

One reason for the importance of observing informal group relations is that informal coalitions arise in every formal group. Some of these, such as "coffee buddies," friendship groups, and the like, have little or no significant impact. But others, such as clique, protest, or resistance groupings, can prevent cohesion and tear morale asunder by their divisive efforts. Often these groups operate against the leader or against other subgroups in a clandestine manner. They may seek to destroy or dilute the team's norms, objectives, values, and philosophy as well as those of the leader.

Your job as manager is to face these group processes when they are adverse to group interests, harmful to individuals, or counterproductive toward goals. You can deal with them by the very act of recognizing them, exposing them for all to see, or finding strategies to break them up. You will never be entirely free of the burden of considering and confronting the ever-changing rise and fall of special interest groups among members of your team.

Coping with Opposition

One of the most serious tasks of a leader in a group is to cope with external and internal opposition to his goals, ideas, or activities. He must learn when to be a graceful loser or a generous winner. He learns to accept, at times, what he doesn't like for the sake of broader gains. He does not fear opposition or criticism and is not afraid to show disapproval of the members of his team. Finally, he has a realistic awareness of the emotional as well as the logical nature of humans.

In most organizations there are loners who can't or won't merge themselves into a team in any real sense. They don't want to share the credit or to rely on the help of peers. Loners often disturb or anger team workers and tend to drift away from organizations too tightly knit to tolerate them for long. Every organization needs a few loners who may be "young Turks" or demanding change agents. Fortunately, there are many who strongly need others, so that they are willing to play on the team and to share the work and the credit.

Cliques and coalitions also pose a threat to the leader's efforts to weld the group into an effective team. To illustrate this consider the case of a bank with a general manager, eight loan officers, ten tellers, and six clerical employees. Let us say that loan officers A, B, and C are opposing a given policy and that they have formed a clique for the purpose of getting rid of the policy. These same three men have been a continuous clique for several months, lunching and taking their coffee breaks together and playing golf on weekends. The policy rebellion focuses the manager's concern on this clique because it represents a threat to his control of the system. Their opposition to the policy has recently been manifested in some apparent but not flagrant failures to apply the policy as intended. The clique may be viewed as a subsystem attached to the greater system and also a system itself.

What should the manager do? What further information does he need? How should he handle this situation? The manager may first consider the technical system and whether the members of this clique have support from the technical factors covered by the policy. They could be right in their views against the policy.

Assume that the technical system is not logically at fault in this situation. What then? The manager faces the need to examine the operation of the clique as a social system. He then notes that the three loan officers have not actually declared their intention of getting rid of the policy. His feelings are based on observing their close personal ties and their individual actions that appear to avoid or distort the application of the policy. It is possible that a clique may arise and be destroyed by the manager without the manager, the clique members, or others in the organization openly acknowledging its existence.

He next considers whether to deal with the clique as a group or with its members as individuals. Now we need to know what his personal relationships with the individuals are. Presumably these vary with each of the three loan officers. He could perhaps take steps to recapture the loyalty and compliance of one or two of the clique members. This amounts to breaking up the clique as a functioning system.

A crucial decision is whether or not to take overt action to break up the clique and, if so, by what means? What are the risks of destroying the clique? It might cost him one or two resignations, depending on how strong his methods were and whether the clique members see themselves losing a whole war rather than merely a battle.

If he cannot break up the clique through his personal relationships with the men, he could use administrative means, such as transfers, withholding wage increases, and the like. He could appoint the clique to a committee to investigate the problems and rely on the technical system to assert its validity over the social system and on the powers of persuasion of other more loyal committee members. Ideally he would use means sufficient to his purpose but no more than sufficient.

Actually, he does not really need to fear this clique; he can probably easily break it up or blunt its efforts, perhaps even before any of the other organization members are aware of its existence. Cliques that endure, however, may seek to recruit new members, which adds to the reasons for breaking them up.

The manager's main objective should be to blunt the impact of the clique's anti-policy activity. He need not necessarily destroy the social system represented by the clique, although destroying the friendship basis of the clique would be the surest way of destroying the clique itself.

A confrontational tactic might be used. The manager could openly point out to the three individuals his awareness and disapproval of their behavior. He could ask them to follow the policy despite their unwillingness to support it and he could stress consequences of their continued concerted resistance to the policy. Direct confrontation, however, might transfer clique action to another area, evoke subterfuges, or cause more decisive action on their part. His problems could begin again. Or a full-scale war might open up.

The manager could well consider the underlying reasons for the formation of the opposition clique. The clique may be meeting expectations not met by the system as a whole. Destroying the clique, therefore, would not solve the deeper problems of dissatisfaction in the group but would only lead to the formation of new cliques.

Leading the Team

There is a great deal of difference between a collection of individuals and a finely built, cohesive work team. Groups, such as the people riding in a subway car, have no leadership. They have little or no awareness of each other or of themselves as a group. It is only when a number of individuals perceive and define themselves as a group that the maximum possibilities for collective effort can begin to be realized.

So leadership is essential to building the team. This will challenge your resourcefulness and creativity. As a leader you are different in degree from your followers, not different in kind. You have many of the same interests, qualities, and capabilities but in greater amounts. The members of the group expect the leader to lead, to be ahead of them, to be different. One corporation president said "I don't particularly like my Jaguar, but I drive a Jaguar as a symbol of my status as head of a great organization. The people in my organization expect me to behave according to their image of a leader." Of course, this president had other qualities too—ideas, vision, technical knowledge, experience, and 100 percent of the stock.

The need for a harmonious, cohesive work group need not make the leader attempt to be "one of the guys" by acting just like ordinary members of the group. He and his followers need mutual respect for each other. Friendliness is not precluded, but the leader needs to keep his demeanor sufficiently impersonal in order to preserve his ability to act rationally and objectively. Undue displays of emotion can undermine a leader. Anger, hostility, vindictiveness, and panic directed toward individuals or the group can detract from the leader's influence.

Continued feuds, bickering, and backbiting can also weaken the leader. He should not allow them to continue unchallenged, or to grow in intensity. Effective leaders directly confront problems in the group. Yielding to expediencies rather than coming to grips with issues will reduce respect for the leader of a group. An example is found in the way a manager may adopt easy, rule-of-thumb policies, such as "first-come, first-served."

The effective leader demonstrates poise, self-control, and equanimity under a variety of trying circumstances. He refrains from gossip, idle small talk, and betrayal of confidences placed in him. He stays out of the limelight, helping others to get the credit which perhaps he deserves. He tries to maintain a sense of proportion in his administrative duties and avoids making mountains out of molehills. He keeps a balanced perspective between short-run, temporary crises and the problems of the future.

The leader sees the shades of gray that pervade all issues. He mistrusts configurations that are all or none, black or white. He avoids stereotyping problems or people.

What happens when the team spirit comes to live in a group has been trenchantly expressed by L. E. Sissman:

> What seems to happen is that the pooled egos of the team members create something greater than the sum of its parts—a detailed, foolproof solution to problems, say, that no member could think through for himself. A creative problem-solving team on the verge of an answer is a stimulating thing to behold and be part of. Each member subjectively makes a contribution. Every other member instantly reacts to this suggestion, but if the group's working right, not in a selfish or egocentric way. Every other member, in short, adds either his objectivity to an evaluation of the suggestion or his creative subjectivity to an improvement on it. . . . At moments like this—moments of breakthrough—every member of the group feels pride in the emerging solution and an exhilaration that can be described only as being off the ground.*

*L. E. Sissman, "What I Gave at the Office," *Atlantic Monthly,* April 1972, p. 7.

CHAPTER
7

Helping Your Subordinates Grow

Working *with* the individuals you supervise is one of your primary challenges as a manager. Working *for* these same individuals may be a new idea to you, although years ago it was epitomized in the phrase "bottom-up management." In essence, this point of view turns the organization chart upside down to dramatize the responsibility a manager has to help subordinates develop their capabilities.

To work effectively with subordinates, you need to concentrate on four managerial activities: knowing each person as a unique individual, dealing with problem people, appraising each person's performance and providing feedback, and assisting each person in planning his training and career development.

Knowing Your Employees

Getting to know your subordinates is a never-ending process. No one can completely know another person because personalities are too complex and people change. Also some resist the efforts of others to know them; they like to keep their private lives private.

Your managerial "need to know" is a limited need. You are not a psychiatric analyst or a clinical psychologist. You need not invade anyone's privacy beyond his willingness to confide. You do not have to know all there is to know about each individual.

On the other hand, without systematically cultivating a thorough knowledge of each individual, you will be handicapped in helping each person to be an effective member of the team. The strategies you use in working with individuals and with the group you manage may be blunted or rendered unusable without adequate knowledge of each person's relevant characteristics.

The skills you need are those of observing, listening to, and talking with others. These skills require continuous practice with improvement in mind. Unless you have had a lot of training in using the tools and concepts of the behavioral sciences, you may have trouble going beneath the surface in your observations. Without special efforts, it is difficult to understand the emotional and other psychological components of a person's makeup.

Although you are not expected to perform as a trained psychologist or a professional counselor, it is important to know as much as you can about the feelings, beliefs, philosophies, and needs of those around you. Necessarily you often deal with vague, abstract elements rather than with obvious tangibles. This can be scary and uncertain. But you can learn to look beyond surface indications. You will not go wrong if you come to understand your limitations and to know when someone else's help is needed.

Your "need to know" is essentially work or task related. This is the center of your concern. In some cases you may become the close personal friend of one or more of your subordinates, but it is best to try to keep this role separate from your role as manager. Your main objective is not to become everyone's pal, but to manage with an adequate measure of human understanding.

Not all people are alike. Therefore your "need to know" differs from one individual to another. There will be some similarities among the people in a group, but the important data for you are their differences.

The meaningful observation of people is a difficult process. Some persons will be self-protective and unrevealing. Some will hide behind a facade. Some may display false, distracting clues or distort your observations by their defenses. Others will be frank, open, and communicative. Few are actually so transparent as to make your knowledge-gathering process an easy one.

Your information may be obtained not only by observation but by specific inquiry. Your inquiries may be formal or informal. Valuable information is often obtained casually and unexpectedly, the product of your ongoing relationship with each individual. Frequency of interaction is important. The more frequent your contacts, the more you can observe and learn. Frequent interaction will also improve the accuracy and certainty of your knowledge, since consistencies and inconsistencies of behavior will be more apparent.

Interviewing and holding conversations are two different processes. From both, you learn, but interviewing is generally more formal and more purposive. In an interview you have objectives in the form of specific information you want to get or give. Through conversations, you learn much of value even apart from the specific purpose of the conversation. In the formal interviews, too, much valuable knowledge may be the by-product of the interview content itself.

Learning to listen is one of the most important skills in getting to know your subordinates. You have to learn to hear symbolically as well as literally. There are two types of content in what people say: the manifest and the latent. The manifest is the obvious factual or substantive content. The latent content contains the more subtle implications, the hidden significance of what is said or done. For example, a subordinate may have the habit of making jokes or wisecracks when criticized. This is manifest content. To understand the individual at a deeper level, you search for the latent content. Perhaps joking is a cover for something the person doesn't want you to notice. It may be a mechanism of defense or a way of hiding hostility or fear. To find the latent content of a subordinate's behavior you may have to make your observations over a period of time. Even then, you cannot always be sure you are right. While you cannot always take people's actions or words literally, neither can you jump to farfetched conclusions.

An important technique for getting at latent content is to draw out the other person fully. Get the individual to talk at length by asking questions or by nodding in agreement to encourage his willingness to talk. Interested silence often helps. If you have over time built up an atmosphere of trust and confidence, you will find it easier to draw others out.

You will need to use extreme care in the handling of information about your subordinates. You should have a policy, communicated clearly, of never disclosing anything you know about a person to any other person. Thus subordinates learn from experience that what they reveal to you is kept confidential.

The Problem Employee

About 80 percent of your subordinates will seldom pose more than minor or infrequent problems for you. The other 20 percent may be your constant concern as problem employees. It is important to work hard on the problems of this 20 percent.

It is also important to distinguish between a problem employee and a troublemaker. The term "troublemaker" implies deliberate strategies to cause trouble for you or for other workers. Many subordinates are problem employees without making a deliberate attempt to cause trouble.

Avoid using the troublemaker label to dismiss problems of your subordinates. Every individual who works for you presents one or more problems for your managerial attention. Each person's patterns are uniquely different. Therefore, with every individual, you face some pluses and some minuses.

Because the behavior of a troublemaker is "different," many bosses don't know how to tackle the problem. Many are afraid to, so they avoid it and it gets worse. Without playing psychiatrist, you have a responsibility to yourself, to the individual, and to the others in your work group to confront the problem directly and promptly.

The first step is to let the genuine troublemaker know you are not afraid of confrontations. Make your limits of tolerance and your expectations clear. Study the person carefully to see if you can discern the causes of adverse behavior. Work to achieve an improvement by getting at the real problem not just the surface one. After reasonable efforts fail, consider separating the genuine troublemaker from the organization.

The "troubled" employee is a different kind of a problem from the troublemaker. However, the reason an individual becomes a troublemaker is often because he is a troubled employee. Troubled employees are more numerous and require much managerial skill to help so that the organization can avoid losing good people.

With troubled or highly troublesome employees, there is no need, and in fact there may be grave difficulties, in trying to do more than you are qualified to do. You are not a psychiatrist or a psychologist, but you may be able to serve a helpful function as a counselor. You need to be aware of your limitations and to make appropriate referrals when additional expertise is required. Most communities and organizations have specialists upon whom you and the troubled person may call.

The counseling process involves the skills of listening more than skills of giving advice. There may be times when it is appropriate for you to advise a subordinate but advice giving has pitfalls. Much advice is never followed, and often it is not welcome. Moreover, it is easy to rely on this process to solve problems, which it rarely does. Even though you may clearly see the wisdom and relevance of your advice, the subordinate may not. The troubled employee has to work problems through himself to find satisfactory solutions. After all, the individual is the one who has to live with the decision.

Closely listening to the problem employee has the advantage of catharsis: he feels better after expressing feelings, telling the story, or venting opinions. When a person asks for specific advice in some area in which you feel competent, you may properly offer it. But for the most part, your counseling effort is founded upon a close, trusting, and listening relationship with each subordinate.

Counseling opportunites abound in informal settings as well as in formal ones. Any contact with another person provides a potential counseling situation. However, you cannot force counseling upon the individual. With patience, many troubled employees will recognize their need for counseling. This self-recognition leads to more effective results, either with you or with a professional counselor.

Performance Appraisal

In most organizations today, appraisal of performance is not treated randomly or casually. Systematic and regular procedures govern the process in order to achieve consistency of results and to maximize its constructive use.

It is imperative to understand that appraisal and evaluation of people is a necessary, continuous, and unavoidable process whether or not there is a formal system. Many decisions you and others make are dependent upon judgments made about individuals and their work.

The concept of judgment is central to appraisal. This is why the term appraisal is preferred to evaluation. Subjective elements cannot be eliminated from any system of appraisal, but the system attempts to keep subjectivity to a minimum and to control its use when it cannot be avoided. Applicable objective data are of course incorporated into the appraisal results. Most appraisal systems try to build in as many objective measurements as possible.

An initial critical task is to fit your appraisal work into the system imposed by organizational policy. If your organization has no uniform policy or program, you are completely on your own. But if a program and its policies exist, you must tailor your appraisals to them even though the organization's program may or may not fit your needs or philosophy of management. In many cases, the established system imposes minimum requirements, with some latitude given for variation. In others, the manager adapts to an imperfect plan. If the plan is bad, you should work toward changing it.

Whatever the system, you have the opportunity to observe certain guidelines that maximize the possibilities for success. They are: making an effort to be fair, consistent, and impartial; setting clear standards or criteria concerning your expectations; and using feedback procedures to generate improvement of job performance.

Unfairness generally derives from accommodating your own biases and allowing them to distort your judgment. It can result from carelessness or inattention to detail, undue haste, your faulty or sporadic observation, or the vindictive desire to "get" someone. It is manifested in judgments made with incomplete or erroneous observations. Unfairness can also result from distorting an appraisal system to fit your own preferences.

Your clue to unfairness will probably be a complaint from an individual who feels unfairly treated. There arc, however, sub-ordinates who will not voice their complaints. They may continue to nurse a grudge against you or the system and to engage in behavior detrimental to themselves and the group. You need to look for signals that reflect feelings of unfair treatment as well as to face forthrightly those who do complain. To analyze such problems start with yourself, then proceed to assess the case brought by the other person.

Setting the standards of criteria for your appraisal procedures is of critical importance. Perhaps the system itself provides basic criteria, such as personality traits, performance results, and quality of work. These may be on rating scales or built into the system of job expectations through job descriptions, delegation, or other means. Even though criteria are listed in some document or device and seem to be spelled out rather completely, you cannot assume that everyone understands them clearly. What counts is the way things work out in practice. Words used to describe behavior or traits to be appraised may not be understood in the same way by everyone involved. Different managers may use them inconsistently among the members of his group. The test of this is in the application.

The selection and use of criteria for appraisal is the greatest weakness in most appraisal systems. Semantic problems abound, and it is difficult to find and apply truly objective, clearly communicated standards. There are at least five main areas which are the focus of standards for appraisal: performance, skills, personality, motivation, and health. Even these vary in their relevance, applicability, and objectivity.

Of all these areas, performance is the most important. As a boss, you want results. Also, it is the most objective base upon which you can build your appraisal. It is the core of "management by objectives" programs which relate appraisal to performance targets mutually agreed on by boss and subordinate. Performance is an entirely legitimate expectation on your part, unclouded by questions of a less tangible nature. No job is immune to having performance standards, though in some jobs such as teaching, being company president, and so on, performance is difficult to specify in entirely objective terms.

Next comes the area of skills. These are important because

they may account for the level of performance. Skills are a necessary but not sufficient requirement for effective performance because skills alone don't guarantee performance. People can usually acquire new skills needed on jobs and can improve their skills as they acquire experience. By appraising skills over various periods of time, changes either for better or worse can be taken into account. Plans for developing individuals can be made following assessment of their problems in skill areas.

The appraisal of personality traits has serious pitfalls. In earlier years, almost all appraisal systems dealt with personality traits, such as integrity, initiative, or maturity. However, experience has shown that rating scales or other systems built around personality traits are inadequate. Over 18,000 possible personality traits have been identified, indicating the scope of the problem of defining traits and avoiding overlaps. Managers simply cannot rate personality traits fairly or consistently among members of a group. In a well-managed appraisal system, however, managers will consider at least a few personality traits. The guideline is to look for major traits which demonstrate or inhibit job performance. Making the connection between an undesirable trait and its effects on job performance is the crucial factor. What often happens instead is that managers look for traits they themselves admire or dislike and insist that others conform to these biases.

Motivation is one of the relatively intangible factors to assess. What motivates an individual can be considered only by inference from behavior patterns and other information. Motivation is an inner process that helps explain why people do what they do. As an inner process, it is hard to find direct evidence of it or to detect changes in it. In spite of these difficulties, however, you will need to take account of motivation in appraising performance. It is particularly important in trying to assess unsatisfactory performance but less revealing in its clues for satisfactory performance.

Finally, you may wish to appraise matters of health or more specifically, attitudes toward health. Again, your concern with health is related to its effect on job performance. Health supplies drive and energy, and poor health can detract from job performance. Both physical and mental health are important, but mental health is the hardest to deal with. Since a person's health can change, you cannot take it for granted. You can encourage annual physical examinations, insist that vacations be taken, correct conditions that interfere with health, and encourage preventive efforts. Above all, it is important to recognize anomalies— patterns of behavior or events that indicate change or difficulty. Your aim is to help subordinates recognize the importance of health and hygiene and to encourage and support health maintenance.

Health problems become particularly important in the near-40 and over-40 age range. These individuals are likely to be functioning under conditions of stress as a result of being promoted to positions with more responsibilities. As a layman you cannot make medical judgments, but as a boss you can be alert for conditions of strain and pressure and take account of health with respect to job performance.

Training and Development

As manager you influence and control a number of training and development opportunities for the members of your work group. Fortunately most people are favorably disposed toward growth and development in their work. Education still rates high among our cultural and social priorities, and human beings are eager to learn both for personal benefit and for improving their work and careers.

Yet many organizations waste money on training programs that are poorly designed, not wanted, or ineptly conducted. Training per se has little value. Only if training is correlated with appropriate needs and careful program planning will there be maximum benefits to the individual and to the organization.

There are two broad categories of training and development: the general context of working relationships and formal programs designed to meet specific needs. The first category recognizes the learning that takes place on the job, amidst a given organizational climate. Individuals learn continuously, adding to their knowledge, skills, and understandings wherever they find themselves. Things change, so individuals change. Learning through daily experience from the job and the organizational climate is essentially unprogrammed and, hence, not directly managed. But as a manager, you have much to do with how the job and the organizational context relate to the development of subordinates. It is essential that the organizational climate be supportive of and consistent with development plans in the formal sector. Otherwise the training will be unsuitable for the individuals concerned.

The second category, consisting of formal programs designed to help individuals in groups, gives the creative manager many opportunities to improve the organization's capabilities through planned change. Programs may be tailor-made to fit the needs of particular persons. They may also be designed more generally to fit the needs of various groups.

In developing your subordinates, you need to consider how the two main categories of effort, formal and experimental, can best be utilized. A good beginning is to consider your own personal influence, as a leader, from a training and development point of view. People learn from examples set before them, ordinary discourse, and daily events on the job. This means that you can put daily experience to work by recognizing the teaching aspect in your supervision of others. This is known as the coaching process. Every contact you have with subordinates is a kind of learning experience for them and for you.

To be an effective coach, you must intend to be one and to practice the kinds of communication it takes to do the job. You must be willing to talk with subordinates, passing along suggestions, ideas, and even criticisms. Full, frank analysis of your own actions is needed, even if you have to reveal your own mistakes.

The development of subordinates through coaching and experience requires subtle thought, patience, and accurate assessment of the needs and capabilities of each person. It also requires confidence in yourself and the rejection of the insecurity you may feel as subordinates threaten your job by their increased skills and knowledge. Your own insecurity can be reduced by realizing that your organization is likely to reward you as a developer of people.

Part of coaching involves delegating growth-type responsibilities to subordinates. As you delegate gradually increasing responsibilities, the subordinate is guided in the acquisition of vital experiences. You can stretch his capabilities by delegating in such a way that the subordinate reaches out beyond his or your ordinary expectations.

One way to assist the learning process through delegation is to allow subordinates to learn from their mistakes. That is, to stretch their capabilities, you take the risk of their making mistakes, you accept the possibility of error on their part, and you try to ease their fear of mistakes. Though you have to consider the costs inherent in mistakes, this kind of learning is often invaluable.

The costs of learning by mistakes can be reduced by incorporating this experience into formal training programs off the job. One retailing company, for example, uses a computer to train fledgling buyers. Simulation exercises throw the employee into a decision-making situation, after which the computer analyzes the decision and informs the trainee of successes and mistakes. Computerized programs of this type are fully adaptable to many kinds of management or employee training situations.

The use of your organization's formal programs should be a significant part of your plans for developing subordinates. You can also use programs offered by outside organizations, such as public schools, universities, consulting firms, and management organizations. These programs offer flexibility, since you need not make permanent commitments to them. Some are costly, so it pays to make careful evaluations in selecting programs.

In using your own or outside training and development programs, it is critical to begin with the individual needs of your subordinates. You know them best, and you should resist the efforts of training directors or others to cram your people into forced learning situations. You should enroll only those subordinates whose work or careers can clearly benefit and who can return to you with enhanced skills or perspective.

The way you approach a subordinate with a suggestion for formal training can turn him off if you start by talking about his inadequacies or deficiencies. It is better to approach his selection from the positive point of view as a development opportunity and not as a banishment or a corrective action on your part.

Follow-up studies need to be made to ascertain the value of the formal training received. Your organization's training director can help you in these evaluations. Look for changed behavior and improved performance attributable to the training. Of course, these evaluations tend to be highly subjective. By working with training directors you can make your judgments with greater ease and objectivity.

You should also work with your training director to design programs specifically for your group. Most training programs contain courses set up on a continuing basis. They are valuable, but you will ultimately need to design programs expressly suited to your unit's unique training needs.

In the assessment of needs and the selection of programs, you should avoid following fads and climbing on bandwagons. The field of organization development is a burgeoning one, but it is rife with untested concepts, misapplications, waste, and misdirected efforts. For some of the advanced techniques, such as transactional analysis or sensitivity training, there should first be a readiness of the organization to pursue them—a sense of the fitness of things. We have long since learned that the sudden or partial introduction of a complex new technique imposed on an organization operated by old-style philosophies and assumptions can only lead to trouble. Long-range organization-wide planning is essential before embracing the newer concepts of organization development.

The idea of organization development is to develop simultaneously the individuals in the organization and the organization itself. The direction of the development is toward their capabilities for adaptiveness, change, and innovation. It aims to develop change agents, to understand the forces of change in both calm and turbulent environments, and to encourage the fulfillment and achievement of people.

Organization development transcends earlier concepts of training, since it embodies a total conceptualization of the organization. It cannot be done piecemeal or without widespread commitment, particularly from the top echelons.

Employee Expectations

To manage according to the precepts described so far in this chapter, it is helpful to understand the fundamental expectations that employees bring to the job. Their expectations will not always be perfectly fulfilled nor are all the relevant elements under your influence. Awareness of the nature of subordinate expectations, however, gives the creative manager a better perspective from which to work with his subordinates. The following are among the most important expectations:

☐Employees desire to be respected members of an effectively functioning group. They expect the group and its members to be respected by others.

☐Employees are generally aware that they must earn their place within the group, that the group will extend them a status that relates to their actions within it. They expect a status commensurate with their participation in the group.

☐Individuals expect support from their group whether their activities are legitimate or otherwise. They will accept or appear to accept most of the group's norms to obtain this support.

☐Individuals expect to sacrifice some of their individuality in order to become participating members of a system, but they also reserve the right in specific instances to differentiate themselves from the group.

☐Employees expect their daily experiences, tasks, and responsibilities to fit into the social system of which they are a part rather than to operate against the system.

☐Employees expect to derive an identity or an official "self" through their association as members of a social system.

☐Employees relate differently to different persons in the system but expect a certain degree of group cohesion and group solidarity.

☐Through the system, individuals derive the meaning of their work and many of their central life interests.

☐Employee expectations are volatile. They change frequently according to the changing moods and needs of individuals.

☐Employee expectations of the social system have increased greatly over the past few decades. For one thing, the educational attainments of all segments of the population are rising, so that expectations are enlarged through greater employee knowledge. Also, pressure groups, such as unions, call attention to the possibilities that can be obtained from organizations; in fact, they assist some employees in their efforts to obtain more of what they expect. Organizations themselves have often taken the initiative in providing benefits which, once provided, remain a part of the ongoing expectations of employees.

An examination of these expectations should make it clear that managers cannot merely manage individuals. Rather they must use their own social skills and their understanding of group or system behavior to work with individuals to achieve particular goals.

Motivation and Human Needs

An understanding of human needs will serve as a key for the creative manager who faces a bewildering array of prescriptions for motivating subordinates. Need theory provides a central concept around which to integrate what appear on the surface to be diverging or overlapping views underlying almost all approaches to motivation. The major idea behind need theory is that improved motivation lies in changing the total situation rather than in doing things to individuals to make them work harder.

As a boss you are an important component of the situation, but the problem of motivation goes beyond this level. It is a problem of the total organization. Thus, modern motivation theories stress the importance of organizational climate, which in turn is a derivative of the attitudes, philosophies, and beliefs about people that managers express either directly or indirectly.

What is ideally required is a concerted plan throughout the organization, supported and disseminated by top management, to operate the organization in accordance with consistent, up-to-date assumptions about people. Improvements on a piecemeal basis are not likely to work nor are isolated efforts generally fruitful. Nevertheless, if conditions throughout the organization are not propitious for a total approach, you can still develop a creative management style that recognizes the wide range of human needs, dignifies the individual, and opens the system to stimulate the capabilities of your own people.

One of the earliest approaches to motivation may be called the carrot and the stick. In this approach the primary managerial tool is the use of strong rewards for desired behavior and strong, certain punishment for undesired behavior. The fact that this system works only under limited and short-run conditions has led Harry Levinson to call it the "Great Jackass Fallacy." He asserts that to think in terms of carrot and stick means regarding employers and co-workers as little more than jackasses. Levinson, a psychoanalytically oriented consultant, opposes the organizational hierarchy and tight control, and favors goal- and task-oriented structuring and supportive inducements to bring out the best in people. Levinson believes that most of the newer motivational approaches are applied as glorified carrot-and-stick methods. He bases his own approach on deep understanding of people's needs and aspirations.*

You may find situations in which the carrot and the stick seem best. However, your overall approach to motivation should give full attention to the influences of needs as the basis of motivation. Some of the important reasons why needs are important in managing your subordinates are these:

☐Expressed needs may differ from real needs. Employees may not always be aware that their behavior, in large part, represents attempts to satisfy personal needs. Also, they often express their needs in terms that may seem more acceptable to others rather than openly state their real feelings (for example, complaining about salaries when the real problem is a feeling of being treated as a piece of equipment rather than as a human being).

☐The most compelling kinds of needs are social and psychological, rather than physical. Therefore, needs are complex.

☐Psychological and social needs are basic and deep within the human personality. They do not change as rapidly as expressed expectations or overt, day-to-day needs.

☐Employees satisfy needs outside as well as inside the sociotechnical system. They recognize limits in the system for the satisfaction of needs and the meeting of expectations.

☐Managers frequently guess wrong when trying to judge what needs exist among particular employees. Paternalistic managerial behavior may result from the manager's defining needs rather

*Harry Levinson, *The Great Jackass Fallacy* (Cambridge: Division of Research, Graduate School of Business, Harvard University, 1973).

than listening and observing to determine what the employee thinks his needs are.

Newer and more sophisticated approaches to motivation are more complex, more subtle, and more demanding on the time, skills, and energies of managers than the carrot-and-stick method. Two contrasting theories that are worth noting are the expectancy theory and the hygiene theory.

The expectancy theory focuses on the achievement and other needs of people and incorporates the principles that govern how people learn, solve problems, and make decisions. Employees have cognitive expectations which, if met, will lead to a high level of job satisfaction and to favorably motivated behavior.

Along with their expectations, individuals have preferences regarding alternative outcomes. Performance in this view is related to an individual's expectancy that a particular outcome will result from his or her behavior and to the importance of (or preference for) that outcome to the individual. Thus the manager who expects a promotion and has a high preference for achievement will engage in those behaviors that increase the likelihood of achieving a promotion. This process is reinforced by a feedback mechanism whereby the satisfaction stemming from equitable rewards for performance influences the connections between effort and reward.*

The hygiene theory, advanced by Frederick Herzberg, has been widely applied in many types of organizations. It is also known as the two-factor theory because it declares that the factors leading to job satisfaction are different from those leading to dissatisfaction and hence should not be viewed as opposite ends of the same continuum. The factors producing dissatisfaction are called hygiene factors. They cause an individual to be dissatisfied if they are not present, but they can only motivate that person to a state of no dissatisfaction. Satisfiers do not cause a person to be dissatisfied when not present, but they provide the manager with his primary way of building high performance through job satisfaction.

---

*Victor H. Vroom, *Work and Motivation* (New York: John Wiley & Sons, 1964).

Dissatisfiers include such things as company policy and administration, supervision, peer relationships, working conditions, salary, and relationships with subordinates. Satisfiers include opportunity for achievement, recognition, the work itself, responsibility, and opportunity for personal growth.*

This two-factor view remains controversial, since it runs counter to the traditional view that satisfaction and dissatisfaction are the opposite ends of a continuum, and since the research to date is inconclusive. Nevertheless, expectancy theory and the two-factor theory represent advances from the more traditional carrot-and-stick methods. What the newer theories of motivation have in common is that they point to the superiority of positive, need-fulfilling approaches over the hard-nosed, carrot-and-stick approaches. They point to the importance of the context in which the superior and subordinate perform and the value of attempting to change the situation as well as the individual. For example, the two-factor theory has stressed job enrichment as a way of redesigning jobs to restore the challenges that were removed by overspecialization.

The creative manager is an obstacle remover not an obstacle maker. He motivates by removing barriers to effective performance, as well as by creating conditions favorable to performance. He constantly asks himself and his subordinates, what can I do differently or stop doing that will help individuals achieve better results?

*Frederick Herzberg, Bernard Mausner, and Barbara B. Snyder, *The Motivation to Work* (New York: John Wiley & Sons, 1959).

CHAPTER
8

How to Achieve More Effective Results

Achievement, for many people, is habit. Once they learn the knack, they continue doing it for a lifetime. The habit is acquired through long, arduous practice and through continuous learning from experience.

The minimum condition necessary for achievement is energy coupled with constructive goals and ambitions. Energy alone won't work. Ambition without ability or energy won't work. Ability, energy, and suitable goals (ambition) must come together in a setting of opportunity to reach fruition in achievement.

We are living in a land of opportunity endowed with individual freedoms as well as challenging problems. We have an immense variety of organizations in which to practice the arts and skills of management. In such a context, achievers can find their niche in worthwhile endeavors.

Making the Most of Yourself

The fact that no one can give you a formula for personal success or for organizational achievement should not deter you from thinking about the problem of self-development. Self-development is founded upon self-understanding. This, in turn, requires planning on your own behalf.

Everyone has both weak and strong points, desirable and undesirable personality traits. It is important to come to terms with oneself to recognize the qualities that must be changed or over-come and the strengths that can be emphasized and better utilized.

Every individual is embarked on a quest for identity. It is a quest because the conditions by which identity is realized are constantly changing. We achieve our identity in many complex ways but chiefly by the qualities we bring to life as a human being. We behave so as to satisfy needs, to fulfill our aims, and to meet the expectations of others. Our behavior tells others what we seek to be or to become, and those others reflect back to us what we call our identity.

Every person desires distinction and uniqueness through the use of his own creative powers and talents. He wants to be ful-filled. This process of achieving fulfillment is one of growth and maturation of the inner self and the personality. A mature person is always clarifying his ideas, learning from a changing environ-ment, and enlarging his capabilities. He responds to change with adaptiveness, resourcefulness, patience, and creativity.

Thus the creative manager is creative with respect to the qual-ities of life and character he seeks to develop within himself. He is creative in directing his ambitions toward better craftsmanship and toward improving some particular aspect of his life. He looks creatively at the ordinary in life, seeks new uses for the old, and highlights that which is hidden to others. The act of creation does not bring forth something out of nothing; it uncovers, selects, reshuffles, and synthesizes already existing facts, ideas, or skills.

Self-knowledge aids a manager in becoming a more successful leader. But every person tends to be somewhat blind to the nature of his own character and personality. Everyone should adopt the habit of self-analysis, self-examination, for, as the So-cratic tenet says, "The only life worth leading is the examined life." With reflection, we can gain insight and awareness. By listening more carefully to others, we can see ourselves as others see us. By practicing the skills of observation, we can learn more about ourselves and others. Greater self-knowledge helps you to pull your best qualities together to form a more unified, inte-grated whole.

Creative efficiency is as dependent upon your quality of driv-ing power as it is upon knowledge and talent. You have known persons who have buried their talent, lost their momentum, allowed their knowledge to evaporate and their skills to deteriorate. "The song that I came to sing remains unsung. . . . I have spent my days in stringing and unstringing my instrument," is a statement by Sir Rabindranath Tagore that beautifully expresses this thought.

Thus, it is apparent that strategies not only face outward toward others but inward toward oneself. The underlying strategy is to be yourself. This means facing honestly the question of what kind of person you really are. Doing this successfully means that you avoid excessive conformity and following temporary fads and fashions. Flattery and bootlicking are obsequious strategies that may be tempting but foreign to your nature. Creativity, courage, and conviction may not make you popular, but in the long run they attest to your belief in yourself.

Following your instincts for uniqueness and your willingness to avoid the common and the ordinary can heighten the effects of all your creative strategies. As soon as you become the predictable person, you have put yourself under the spell of your adversaries' strategies.

Communication

You've been told so much about communication already that you surely must be wondering why you should hear more about it in this book. The reason is simple: communicating remains one of the most important single human skills the manager needs.

Despite all the attention given to the improvement of communications, it is clear that the level of effective communication among most people in an organization is extremely poor. Yet communication is a skill that can greatly aid one's development if one puts systematic effort into its improvement.

To see the scope of your communication problem, think for a moment about your typical workday. How many people need to interact with you to get their jobs done? How many people do you need to contact in getting your work accomplished? How much communication is generated for you by the communications of others? You will find that, like most managers, you spend 60 to 80 percent of your time each day in a communications

process or situation. Almost everything you do involves com
munication in some form or other.

The basis for communication is words, either written or spo-
ken. But words are symbols that refer to objects or ideas; their
function is to convey meaning. Meaning in turn derives to a large
extent from context, with includes the signs and signals of facial
expressions, gestures, and body postures. Thus communication
is a function of the total process of interacting with others.

The use of language is a tricky business. In your written communications, your words stand alone. They don't have the support of your presence, facial expressions, or gestures. Therefore
in written messages you have to say what you mean, and mean
what you say. A cogent, clear, and simple style is needed, and
you can develop such a style through practice and analysis. Even
professional writers make the effort to keep improving.

A favorite dodge for those who can't write or spell is to turn the
job over to a secretary or the company editor. While it is wise to
recognize the value of such help, it does not absolve you of the
responsibility you bear for the content and clear transmission of
the messages you originate.

Both written and oral communications are too often loaded
with clichés, jargon, and empty language. Clichés are catch
phrases that have lost their meaning and cogency through over-
use. Too much repetition of trite phrases numbs the message
receiver, and deprives you of uniqueness by making you sound
like everybody else. Consider, for example, the frequently used
phrase, "more fun than six monkeys in a rainbarrel." This cliché
is obviously devoid of meaning in most situations in which it is
used.

Jargon greatly debilitates the communications process. It is
"trade language" developed to obfuscate those not privy to it.
The social sciences are full of jargon by which social scientists can
talk to each other but not to outsiders: hidden agenda, status-
seeker, exurbanite, meritocracy are examples. If you are a
lawyer, engineer, or other specialist you are in danger of hiding
behind jargon to the distress of those to whom you want to clearly
communicate something. Vacuous or weak language abounds in
organizational message-sending while, at the same time, vital
information is excluded. Important dates, deadlines or other facts

are omitted while vague words hide the real intent of messages.* Most communication problems center on the lack of sensitivity of the communicator to the needs and situation of the message receiver. It is natural for the communicator to put his own interests and intentions first, without considering the emotional connotations and nonrational considerations inherent in most communications situations.

To summarize, you can improve your managerial effectiveness by devoting attention to the following factors:

Avoid clichés and weak, empty language.

Guard your use of jargon in general communications situations.

Simplify your oral and written expressions.

Tell everything you should tell to all who have the need to know.

Check the timing of your communications to make sure you are informing others appropriately.

Consider the emotional and other psychological implications of every communication.

Be aware that you are conveying a reflection of yourself as well as a specific content.

Polish your writing style for clarity, simplicity, brevity, and coherence.

In oral communication, the great art of listening is the most frequently violated principle. Listening requires interested attention and patience. The creative manager listens at two levels: the manifest and the latent. The manifest level conveys the actual message content, the literal meaning. The latent content conveys the hidden, more subtle meaning of a communication. Clues to latent meanings are given by gestures, body postures, facial expressions, and inflections of voice. Repeat the phrase "good morning" with different inflections and you will see that it can mean either a cordial greeting or a sour, ironic "bad morning."

The benefit of listening is not yours alone. The communicator who is listened to "gets things off his chest" and feels better by receiving an attentive, sympathetic, sincere, and interested hear-

---

*An instructive and enjoyable work to read on this subject is Edwin Newman, *Strictly Speaking* (Indianapolis: Bobbs-Merrill, 1974).

ing. Letting your subordinates and colleagues "unload" in this way can do much to improve their regard for you. However, willingness to listen, if uncontrolled, may have its drawbacks. A completely open-door policy may not work well. Subordinates may be reluctant to barge in. If you are not in fact an easygoing, jovial person, you can't pretend to be. If you are busy, you cannot and should not hide this fact. Without careful listening, however, you are likely to receive only the messages people want you to hear, shutting you off from the undesirable things people want to keep you from knowing. If people avoid communicating with you, it could be due to your behavior, or to their strategies. It could also be due to organizational constraints such as layers of organization structure, physical inaccessability, lack of privacy, or obvious status symbols.

Obviously you need a good feedback. Getting reliable feedback is difficult because there is ample opportunity for distortion or withholding. The feedback principle holds that you can appraise the value or utility of a communication or a decision by receiving information about it from others or from the reactions to it. You can then change or adjust by applying the information received as feedback. The principle is similar to that of the household thermostat that regulates room temperature. But feedback can be dangerous to an organization if it results in phony data. Betsy and Gabriel Gelb have described forced, fuzzy, and filtered forms of feedback. Feedback is forced when it results from social or organizational pressure. A subordinate asked about results of a project in front of peers is forced to lie or stretch the truth to maintain their respect. A fuzzy answer, such as saying "the project is in good shape" when it really isn't, is a defense ploy. Feedback is often filtered as it passes upward in an organization. Reports get better as they go up. The supervisor says, "Our scrap reports look bad." His general manager says, "Our scrap reports are below normal." The department head says, "Our scrap reports are better this month than last." The vice-president says, "Our scrap reports are improving."*

Your strategy on feedback should not be to force it but to

*Betsy D. Gelb and Gabriel M. Gelb, "Strategies to Overcome Phony Feedback," *MSU Business Topics*, Autumn 1974, pp. 5-7.

encourage it, to reward useful feedback and act upon it, to make firsthand observations to check on or avoid relying on feedback, and finally, to feed back the feedback—report on the results of feedback so they can guide those affected.

Solving and Preventing Problems

Being a good problem solver is the way to personal success, right? Wrong! While it is always good to be able to solve a problem, a more subtle art is that of preventing problems, at least the serious ones.

Problems are essentially prevented by foresight and good planning. This entails the imaginative consideration of the consequences that are likely to follow from decisions made and actions taken. It is the undesirable, unintended consequences that create additional problems, and these are the most difficult to predict. Often, however, they are not predicted because decision makers are so eager to decide that they do not really listen to the sources of information that might dissuade them.

Some managers specialize in creating problems which only they can "solve," thus cultivating a heroic image of their capabilities. There are times when you may be forced to be a creator of problems for others or for yourself, but such situations usually are valuable only if they result in ultimate, long-run benefits. Creating problems for the sake of creating problems is an expensive hobby.

While problem prevention is one of your main goals, problem solving remains a contender for your time and effort. No organization, no leader, is without problems. The first step is to recognize a problem when it exists. Many people are tempted to hide or ignore problems, with the result that things get worse. Real problems seldom go away by themselves.

The form in which you recognize a problem is also important. For creative action, the problem needs to be formulated in action terms, not merely in a descriptive way. The terminology of the problem, logicians say, determines the terminology of the solutions. Moreover, priorities and interrelationships among problems need to be considered. A one-at-a-time approach can keep

you overwhelmed for years and allows no room for the prevention of future problems or of reoccurrences. To illustrate, consider absenteeism. If you define it as a control problem, your
answers tend to focus on punishment or disciplinary action and
assume that the trouble is caused by wayward, indifferent employees. If you define the problem as one of morale and motivation, you thereby ascribe at least part of the cause to the organizational and managerial context, and you come up with broader,
more inclusive solutions that recognize the interplay between
the individual and the organization.

The consolidation of several small problems with similar causes
or manifestations can lead to solutions that are more broadly
applicable and more likely to prevent other more serious problems. It avoids the conflict you can create by solving smaller
problems one at a time.

The sources of problem formation provide an intriguing game
for analysis. First there are the problems that you yourself create
or define. You see them in your role as a leader. You may have to
convince others with less information that a problem exists in the
form you describe it.

A second source is problems others bring to you. They may
have to convince you of the problems' existence or importance.
Problems may come from outsiders, such as customers or government regulators. Others come from peers and subordinates.
Naturally you have to evaluate their problem statements and fit
them into the larger picture.

The basic questions for an organization are: Which problems
can it tolerate? Which should it recognize? and Which should it
try to eliminate? A well-recognized, serious problem about which
everyone is in general agreement can remain for years untouched
by administrative action. This happens when other problems are
even more serious, when solutions require resources that are not
available, or when managers are indifferent to its effects.

In most cases, you will not be solving problems alone. Most
problems encompass several echelons of the organization or cut
across departments and functional units. Such problems need
work by teams, task forces, or committees. Even within your
own domain, problems need efforts of everyone affected by them
or by those who have important inputs. The leader who can tap

the abilities of his followers is thereby strengthened in his leadership.

Great pressures on problem solving come when time is short or the stakes are large. The ability of a group to solve problems depends on its information gathering and on alternatives assessment, which in turn are a function of the time and money available. There is seldom time for achieving perfect or optimum solutions. You have to be content with reasonable solutions in a reasonable amount of time at a reasonable cost.

Leadership

Leadership today is considered to be a situational phenomenon rather than solely a set of personal traits possessed by individuals. Of course, personality traits, experience, and technical skills have a bearing, but these result in leadership to a degree highly dependent on the organizational context. So it is upon the interaction between the manager as an appointed "leader" and his followers in a particular set of circumstances that we must focus attention.

You can manage without leading by simply administering the status quo. By contrast, the idea of leadership implies a forward, progressive direction of change. If change is minimal or impossible, leadership is an empty slogan. The leader is essentially an effector of change.

The counterpart of situational leadership is charismatic leadership. Charisma is helpful to an appointed leader since it indicates the nature of one's personal influence over others.Through his drive, energy, insight, and personal magnetism, the charismatic leader attracts followers, commanding their respect and knitting them together in concerted action. People become followers in a spirit that transcends strictly rational response. They go beyond the call of duty to help accomplish things. They respect, honor, and admire such a leader.

Charismatic leaders are not numerous, though many appointed leaders may have charisma to some degree. Truly charismatic individuals, such as great political leaders, seem to be born that way, though they may capitalize heavily upon opportunity and circumstance. Fortunately you need not have great charisma to exercise leadership in a formal organization. You can succeed with some charisma plus administrative ability and insight.

We do not know exactly how charisma develops, but it is manifest in the leader's intensity of commitment to missions, objectives, and aims, and in a depth of involvement with people and problems in an organization. Charisma is reflected in the joy of action, the achievement of group purpose, and the subtleties of sensitive, considerate involvement with people in the centers of action.

Situational leadership is a role taken by one or more individuals in particular contexts. The role of actual leadership may pass from one to the other in a group. The demands of the situation evoke leadership roles of complex varieties. In this view, a leader is a person who can influence or prevent the actions of others. As an appointed leader you will come to recognize that others in your group may take leadership roles, and you will gain stature by encouraging them to do so.

A crisis is one good test of an effective leader. You no doubt abhor, as others do, constant management by crisis. Yet even in the best-run organizations, crises will occur. Your ability to remain calm, marshal resources, and mobilize others to action is critical in meeting the test of crisis.

Effective leaders use judgment in the degree to which they differentiate themselves from others, particularly followers. Followers want their leaders to be ahead of them but not too far ahead, and they want them behind them (for support) as well as ahead of them. Leaders who are too far apart from their groups lose touch, and the confidence of followers fades. Such leaders may lose not only their effectiveness but also their status as a member of the group. Followers expect their leaders to be assertive, aggressive, active, sources of new ideas and challenges, and spokemen for innovation and change. But they also expect them to be safe, careful, and secure, wise, and just in their decisions. New ideas and changes must not be too different or too sudden, and a leader's decisions must be similar to those his followers would have made in similar circumstances.

In one sense a leader is also a follower. The story is told of a man who was seen running valiantly after a group of people ahead. "Why are you running after those people?" someone shouted. "I have to follow them. I am their leader," he said.

Thus, effective leaders are not front men, puppets controlled by followers. Rather they are generators of creative action for themselves and others. Leaders are not quick to find fault; they guard their criticisms carefully. They are fact conscious, action-oriented, and able to tone down pent-up emotions when such are counterproductive. They help their group convert antagonisms into positive, constructive action.

The Change-Agent Role

All leaders are change agents, but not all managers are. However, effective managers must be alert to the need to play a change-agent, leadership role.

Staff managers are by definition one of the prime sources of change. They are, by training, experience, and professional technique, equipped both to initiate and activate change. Line managers, too, can initiate and carry out change, with or without the help of staff managers. They can also block changes initiated by staff units. Effective change often depends on close liaison between line and staff managers.

Change requires some of the same skills as leadership. To be a change agent requires a sharp preception of problems, the ability to assess needs for change, the evaluation of change forces in the internal and external environments, and the ability to persuade others and to enlist their help.

The change-agent role, which can be expected of any manager, includes raising the level of awareness of other people about the nature of problems and their possible solutions; helping others avoid oversimplification and improve their diagnosis; suggesting alternatives; providing information; analyzing assumptions and consequences; considering values, beliefs, and philosophies; and improving the skill of observation and analysis.

Consultants

Consultants are specialists of various types who are typically brought in from the outside to develop change and improvement plans. Like staff people, consultants are a type of change agent. Indeed some organizations maintain staffs of full-time consultants who serve various units much the same as outside consultants might.

Outside consultants are needed when equivalent capabilities are not available inside. They are often called in to help with large-scale, complex, or long-run projects, and are used for planning as well as carrying out projects. The presence of a consultant does not necessarily denote the failure, mistakes, or ineptness of existing managers, although this may on occasion be a real or an imagined concern.

Except in unusual circumstances, you should be able to call on consultants yourself when the need arises. You also must deal with consultants when someone else brings them in, and you should have a voice in selecting them if they are to deal in any significant way with your domain of interest. You should follow the practice of learning all you can from consultants and of helping them in their work. Most consultants try to operate through existing managers, serving in an advisory rather than a decision-making capacity. Only when consultants are installing a program or a package system of their own design are you likely to be precluded from actively shaping what they do.

A chief value of the consultant is his role as an outsider with a detached, objective view and no vested interests. The consultant is the possessor of knowledge and experience collected from an array of other organizations, thereby providing a broader base of action.

Some major changes can scarcely be accomplished without the use of an outside change agent or consultant. An example is the major turnaround of an organization's management practice from an authoritarian to a more participative, adaptive, open systems approach. This goal is frequently called "organization development." Its capability for extensive change in a relatively short time is so great, and the need for behavioral science expertise is so critical, that outside specialists are required to take the new methods to the point that permanent managers can continue the changes on their own.

Many questions arise with respect to consultants. When is a consultant needed? Should a large firm or a freelance individual

be selected? What are the consultant's credentials? Is a specialist
or a generalist needed? What qualifications are critical? What
will the work cost? How can the most be gotten out of the consultant? How can the recommendations be applied? These questions indicate the need for careful advance preparation in hiring
consultants.

In a sense you yourself may act in a consulting role when called
on for assistance or advice by units outside your own. Virtually
the same rationales and criteria apply to the inside as well as the
outside consultant.

Conformity

Many organizations expect conformity more than they expect
change because change can be upsetting and difficult. There is
some evidence that most individuals have an inherent tendency
to conform, especially when social or other pressures are applied.
A team of psychologists constructed a test to study this question.

First they drew lines on two large white cards. One card
showed a standard line of certain length. The other card had a
line the same length as the standard line plus two others that
were shorter.

The psychologists placed teams of seven to nine young men in
a room together. All but one of the young men had been coached
in advance. The last man was the subject under study. The men
who had been coached in advance argued hotly that one of the
shorter lines on the second card was as long as the standard line
on card No. 1. They pressed the subject to agree.

The crux of the test was whether the subject—the man not in
the know—would feel forced by social pressure to agree with the
majority opinion, even when he saw that the majority was wrong,
or whether he would insist that the majority had matched up the
wrong lines.

When the man under test was pitted alone against the group
he generally gave in—only 25 percent flatly refused to conform.
But when the test subject was supported in his opinion by even
one other member of the group, he generally held out against the

majority; under these conditions 75 percent of the test subjects refused to alter their views.*

It is helpful to be aware of the possible effects of undue social pressure to conform. Conformity is often safer than departure from norms or expectations. But in conformity you are more like the average person. In being different you stand out from the crowd with an integrity of your own.

*For a review of this and other studies on conformity, see Bernard M. Bass, *Leadership, Psychology, and Organizational Behavior* (New York: Harper & Row, 1960).

CHAPTER
9

Women in the World of Work

All that has been said elsewhere in this book applies equally to both men and women managers, but this chapter focuses on some crucial problems that pertain to women in a world yet dominated by men. The following chapter will examine a special class of problems that arise with respect to working or nonworking spouses.

In the past decade, more than ever before, the contributions of women have attained increasing significance in our society. Despite our progress in reappraising the roles that women can and should play in organizations, however, there is much room for improvement. Most organizations today espouse the value of their "human resources," while at the same time ignoring or overlooking the untapped potentials of female employees.

Women and Work

Discrimination against women, as well as against other groups in society, has been widespread, although much of it has been the result of complicated social and economic factors rather than of deliberate intent. Such discrimination is nevertheless pervasive in the world of work.

Legislation focused on affirmative action programs has resulted in considerable progress in achieving fair employment practices for women. No longer may organizations legally discriminate in hiring, promoting, or rewarding female employees. No longer may they maintain job titles, pay structures, benefits, or other programs with distinctions based on sex criteria. Clearly these new policy requirements greatly alter the work environment and carry extensive implications for the strategies, conduct, and attitudes of all the members of an organization.

In the modern age, women in increasing numbers are advancing in organizational and professional careers, and they are doing so with commensurate improvements in status and acceptance. Many women now occupy positions formerly reserved for men. More and more married women are pursuing relatively permanent working careers, with husbands and wives sharing domestic responsibilities in patterns unfamiliar to men and women of a generation ago.

Increasingly, women will be working for organizations in responsible managerial and technical positions. They will more and more be intent upon following varied, individual, and relatively permanent careers. As educational pipelines improve the training and capabilities of women, they will enter organizations in larger numbers at higher levels, no longer confined to clerical, secretarial, or other routine jobs. Male managers accustomed to the uncompetitiveness and nonthreatening roles of women may have difficult adjustments to make. Women employees, unaccustomed to organizations open to their advancement and providing conditions of equality with men, will also have to adjust to their new opportunities and responsibilities.

In brief, the social structure of working organizations is changing with respect to sex role differentiation. The necessary adjustments for both men and women will be difficult but at the same time rewarding because the new conditions are more harmonious with expectations in society at large.

Women in managerial positions are more frequently found in staff rather than in line jobs. Increasingly they will be competing for line jobs, because the line is where the power centers lie. While staff jobs can be challenging, they emphasize analyzing things rather than supervising people. And research shows that women have special strengths in dealing with people.

A real breakthrough in the realm of progress for career women thus lies in the line segments of organizations, but line roles are difficult for women because men are not used to delegating authority to women, nor are they used to reporting to female bosses. Moreover, stiffer competition with men and other women for line jobs adds to the difficulties that women must face.

Such challenges call for creative managerial action on the part of the aspiring female executive. Younger, newer female executives encounter chauvinism from older women as well as from men. Strategies directed toward their bosses and subordinates are necessary to overcome initial barriers to effective working relationships. Among these strategies are the following (some, of course, apply equally to a new male supervisor):

Proposing mutual goals that shift the focus from role considerations to a results orientation.

Involving others in such a way as to stress mutual gains and interests.

Avoiding drastic and immediate change until relationships are better established.

Avoiding emphasis on formalities and protocols.

Learning not only the work but also the personalities involved.

Cultivating the skills of approachability through continuous interaction.

Finding a balance between submissiveness and aggressiveness.

Avoiding dangerous "sink-or-swim situations."

Accepting full responsibility for her own efforts, relating directly to her subordinates without allowing her own boss to interfere.

Avoiding the need to be frequently "bailed out" by the boss.

Reacting thoughtfully to criticism or failure.

Avoiding the role of "big sister" to subordinates or bosses.

Avoiding extreme efforts to gain rapport at the expense of surrendering authority and responsibility.

Avoiding exploitive maneuvers that rely on feminine wiles.

Changing ideas about women at work in organizations are but one aspect of parallel changes in the role and status of women in society generally. The women's liberation movement has generated new views of women's rights and duties outside the organization as well as inside. As a result, home and family relationships are being altered in ways that affect husbands and wives in their places of work. The creative manager, whether male or female, must take into account these changing social norms together with their impact on their roles and statuses within organizations.

Two critical problems emerge from these changing social norms and organizational conditions. First, there is the problem of overcoming myths, stereotypes, and attitudes which have adverse impacts on women at work. The second problem is the need for men and women managers to adjust to unfamiliar, untraditional organizational relationships which will appear more and more frequently.

Stereotypes, Myths, and Attitudes

Laws by themselves can never fully produce the ideal behavior envisioned by society. As a result creative managers, whether men or women, must carefully think about how to live up to the spirit and not merely the letter of the law. The first step is to release one's mind from the distortion of stereotyped thinking. Not all women are alike, just as not all men are alike. Working women have a variety of motives, just as men do. Every individual represents a particular balance of masculine and feminine traits. Yet stereotypes classify people rigidly according to characteristics that apply, by implication at least, to all members of a group.

Stereotyped thinking by men tends to categorize women as "problems," "weak sisters," or "inferior beings." Women are frequently thought to be without career aspirations, interested mainly in finding husbands, getting a paycheck, or escaping from responsibilities at home. Such stereotypes engender hostility toward women who leave home, reject or delay marriage, nurse career ambitions, or who like to work and who enjoy competing with others. Women, too, are guilty of perpetuating unfortunate stereotypes about men as always "on the make," overly aggressive, unfair, uncommunicative, or selfish. The trouble with stereotypes is that they are rigid notions which do not stand up under close scrutiny when one objectively considers particular individuals at particular times and places.

Closely associated with stereotyped thinking is the tendency of men to accept myths that relegate women to a secondary status. It is, for example, a myth that women cannot endure sustained effort, cannot work hard, do not desire careers, or cannot engage in physical labor. It is also a myth that women *per se* are gossipy, talkative, frivolous, or dumb.

Women maintain the myths that men prefer to be with other men in social settings and at work, that men resist domestication and monogamy, that men dislike family responsibilities, that men don't cry, are hardboiled, fast-paced, interested only in sexual matters, impatient, devious, thickheaded, *et cetera*.

Stereotypes and myths about women are notable for being off the mark. Applied to particular cases, they are distortions which block the effective utilization of female employees. A nationwide study by the Institute for Social Research of the University of Michigan found substantial evidence refuting several myths about women workers. * For example:

Myth: American women work just for "pin money."

Finding: Almost 40 percent of all working women are their families' sole support or earn the bulk of the family income.

Myth: Women would not work if they did not have to.

Finding: Three-fourths of all men and single women said they would work in any case; 57 percent of the married women said they would work even if not for economic necessity.

Myth: Women are more satisfied than men with intellectually undemanding jobs.

Finding: Both men and women are equally dissatisfied with undemanding jobs, but women are more likely than men to have such jobs.

Some stereotyped attitudes attributed to women are not so completely disproved, however. Women did indicate a greater

*Robert P. Quinn and Linda J. Shepard, *The 1972-1973 Quality of Employment Survey* (Ann Arbor: Survey Research Center, University of Michigan, 1973).

preference than men for pleasant physical surroundings and convenient travel to and from work. Women also emphasized the
importance of helpful and friendly co-workers more than did
men.

As with stereotypes, the antidote to mythology is the objective
perception of individuals as individuals. It helps also to recognize
the functions of myths and stereotypes. Stereotypes and myths
about women are designed to comfort men, to enhance their
egos, to strengthen their feelings of security, dominance, and
superiority, and to ward off the threat of their competition.
Stereotypes and myths about men are designed to help women
adjust to male dominance and the superior roles men have enjoyed in society. Clearly a new world is arriving in which myths
and stereotypes about men and women will fade and both will
appear in the world of work on a more balanced, even footing.

Attitudes, too, are important determinants of effective relationships between men and women at work. Men frequently
hold the attitude that "a woman's place is in the home," or that
women are generally inferior beings. They lack respect for
womanhood and believe that chivalry is dead. They believe that
gentlemanly behavior is a sign of weakness, although they also
often think that women are fragile, like flowers. Or they may
hold the opposite attitude that if a woman is going to compete
with men she should be tough, hardboiled, and exhibit masculine traits.

The attitudes of women at work are also important, and not
without fault. Women who display a chip-on-the-shoulder attitude, constantly complain without constructively acting on
their own behalf, hate men, dislike other women, rely on
feminine wiles, or assume excessively masculine traits do their
own cause much harm.

Studies in the U.S. Department of Labor and among large
companies have exploded the belief that women are not stable,
reliable, or permanent members of the workforce. Gradual improvement in child care facilities, better attitudes toward women
in organizations, less social stigma for working women, divorce
rates which increase the number of women as "heads of house-
holds" are all factors that generate stability among women in the
workforce. Increasingly the causes of turnover among women

can be expected to resemble those among men—pay, job satisfaction, working conditions, career advancement, and the like.

High-Level Positions Pose Problems

Women in managerial positions face many problems that men do not have to confront. One is a tendency to be afraid of taking risks, either in changing jobs to advance their careers or in making decisions for their organization. The fear is understandable, since the change or decision that does not work out may be blamed upon their being women. The two concerns are related because the fear of failure limits their chances for moving up.

Women managers, too, often do not share the same reward structure that men do. They tend to be paid in "love and affection" rather than in raises, titles, or money. Their organizations, according to many observers, do not undertake affirmative action programs with the same thoroughness as they undertake a computer installation. And even where women are rising to higher-level administrative positions, they follow ancillary routes rather than direct pathways to key jobs in top management.

Career anxieties of women stem to a large degree from fears that success would bring social rejection and loss of femininity. These feelings are reinforced by the fact that men and women are brought up to see themselves as sexual partners rather than working colleagues. Men and women managers do not pursue the same off-hours social relationships that men experience with other men.

The degree of competitiveness required for a woman's success as a manager may often seem to collide with deep-seated traits of femininity encouraged in our culture. One authority has stated that women will not achieve high positions of extraordinary responsibility until they acquire very strong success motives and are willing to be nonconformist, take risks, and be consumed by the desire to get ahead. Thus there are emotional costs of success which some women are unwilling to pay. Studies show, however, that women are less likely to hide or repress their emotions than men. It is probably healthier to express emotions rather than to bottle them up. If so, women should not find emotionalism an undue handicap unless they use emotions as an exploitive device to get their way.

The following quotations from career women making $22,000 to $37,000 per year in a large metropolitan government organization illustrate how some women balance the need for aggressive, decisive behavior with other considerations:

> I feel like a pioneer. I think that women bring a special sensitivity to government that comes from having been have-nots for so long. We're attuned to people and their problems. . . .
>
> *Director, Public Information Department*

> Tenacity is the hidden weapon. You have to keep plugging away—and you have to have a tough hide.
>
> *Member, Civil Service Commission*

> There is a feeling that women are more likely to just want to get the job done well, without having their name on the project.
>
> *Director, Civil Service Commission*

> You have to hustle. You have to learn to juggle a hundred different things.
>
> *Director, City Planning Department*

> The word aggressive, when applied to women, has always had negative connotations, but you have to be aggressive in pursuit of goals. If you're hesitant or neutral, things won't get done.
>
> *Personnel Director*

> A successful woman has to have what I call grace philosophy. That means accepting that at moments one will be hard and sometimes ruthless—but balancing that with integrity and compassion.
>
> *Director, Municipal Parking**

The Role of Education

The progress of humanity toward the ideal of equality of men and women at work is impeded not only by attitudes within the organizations but also by attitudes and beliefs that pervade society as a whole, particularly as reflected in its educational systems. It is probable that most schools of business and management virtually ignore the woman manager. Cases and text materials are peopled almost entirely with men, and such women who do

---

* *Detroit Free Press*, July 14, 1974, p. 1D; article by Charlotte Robinson.

appear occupy clerical or at best, secretarial roles. Most teachers in business schools are men; the few women in the field teach secretarial work, report writing, and the like. Thus a distorted image is conveyed in the educational process.

Perhaps this distortion lies at the root of another problem— that few women apply for enrollment in such schools, and few are graduates. Until recently the emphasis in higher education has been that women are fitted for certain selected roles, such as music, teaching, or the arts. Few have so far been willing to run counter to accepted images by enrolling in engineering, business, or the sciences. While these delimiting social restrictions are declining, enough remain to remind creative managers to review their own concepts of the opposite sex in order to weed out myths, stereotypes, and chauvinistic attitudes.

Women enter the world of management and the professions both from traditional women's colleges and from private and public coeducational institutions. One research finding holds that women educated at women's colleges tend to achieve significantly more than those from coed institutions. Such a finding may not prove conclusively that women's colleges are better, but it should give pause to the critic who would denigrate them entirely.

In a survey of 10,500 women planning to take the Admissions Test for Graduate Study in Business, the Educational Testing Service queried their reasons for studying the field of business, and what they expected when they achieved their educational goals. The study found that women entering business schools have most of the same characteristics as males but feel that they are in for a tough fight in male-dominated environments. The typical woman seeking a business career is independent, ambitious, and capable of making decisions. According to this survey she wants to be treated equally with men, enjoy freedom in her work, use her special talents, and have a chance to become a leader. However, the women felt that business schools are organized to guide women into fields traditionally reserved for women and that the schools have too few women professors, counselors, and administrators.

Since masculine and feminine roles are culturally and socially conditioned and are deep-seated in people's minds, it will take considerable time to reduce negative attitudes and beliefs and to replace them with constructive counterparts.

New Organizational Relationships

As a manager, whether you are a man or a woman, you must face the possibility of being supervised by a person of the opposite sex. Until recently, the idea that a woman can successfully supervise men would have seemed preposterous. It is now becoming a reality. So too is the situation in which a male manager directs the work of female managers or supervises women who are doing what was formerly "men's work."

Until now, discrimination has taken the form of strongly defined and rigidly categorized jobs, those suitable for females and those for males. These distinctions are now banned by law and are no longer as rigid as they once were. However, discrimination difficulties for women continue on three fronts: the level at which they enter an organization, the problem of promotion, and the matter of pay.

Organizations simply have not become used to the idea of female job applicants qualifying for middle management or higher management positions. The practice has always been for women to start at clerical or secretarial levels or some other lower-level position. If they were good, they could work up to administrative assistant, executive secretary, or perhaps office manager. Similarly, some occupational categories were deemed more suitable for women than others, such as nursing, beauticians, or retail store clerks. By not having access to middle management level positions, women miss out on both the formal and informal training and development structures so valuable to the aspiring male employee. This is the level at which specialist training gives way to generalist training and one's personal contacts and gamesmanship really begin to count. Thus to deprive women of entry to this group by promotion or initial hiring is to bar them from rising to meaningful positions higher up.

Discriminatory pay practices flout the law, but they continue despite lip service to the principle of "equal pay for equal work." Pay differentials heretofore have been justified by claims that money is not as important to women as to men; women are only temporary or fickle employees; women are not family breadwinners; women are more costly employees due to illness, high turnover, longer training, or temperamental behavior. These claims are readily seen to be further examples of myths, stereotypes, false attitudes, and rationalizations.

A lone woman working with a group of men has particularly difficult problems. One study found that men tend to ignore a lone woman in a group. They reject her efforts to take an active role. If she reacts with anger or emotion of any kind, they dismiss her as temperamental or neurotic. The findings of this study suggest that the presence of one woman interferes with the mechanisms by which a male group works. Men fear that the woman will act weak, play on their sympathies, or compete successfully with them. Men need to face their fears and hostility to the woman but are barred from doing so by taboos against openly expressing them. For the woman, it is best to be part of a group that includes at least two or three women. Otherwise she may have to accept the role of social isolate, enlist outside support, or play the role of weak sister—a role the men will respond to but may not respect.*

It may be that women are "too honest for their own good," as one consulting psychologist put it. She found that many women are too candid, too direct in speaking up and naming names in criticism. It takes considerable experience to realize that frankness isn't always appreciated. Women can be their own worst enemy by their lack of discretion and skill in the game of company politics. According to another psychologist, "Women aren't as forceful, assertive, and confident as men in similar situations." Tests show that in a group of men and a group of women of equal intelligence, men will score better in dominance and assertiveness. Women score higher on the scales measuring emotion. Doing things the political way has little to do with brains or talent.†

*Based on a report in"Newsline" column, *Psychology Today*, February 1973, p. 10.

†*Chicago Daily News*, "Is Honesty the Best Policy for Working Women?" CDN release dated August 22, 1975.

The fact that women may be their own worst enemies, without strong self-images, was brought out in a questionnaire given to the female employees of a large corporation, who were in clerical, minor management, or professional jobs. To the direct question, "Do you prefer a male or female boss?" 67 percent answered male. Yet only 36 percent thought men make better supervisors than women. * In another study, preference for male bosses was found to be less in the under-25 age group. Only 46 percent preferred a male boss, 18 percent wanted a female boss, and 36 percent said it didn't make any difference.†

Some traditional ideas about the secretary-boss relationships are also changing. More males, for example, are seeking secretarial and clerical positions. Female secretaries are frequently achieving higher status as "administrative assistants," and are finding more doors open for attaining beginning-level positions in management. This leads to more turnover and a tighter labor market in clerical and secretarial positions.

Secretaries often play a key role in the success of their bosses but without commensurate recognition or reward. Too frequently, their bosses treat them as mere errand runners or personal servants. One nationwide survey of 1,000 secretaries found that their opinions ranged from "anything the boss wants is O.K." to "getting coffee for the boss is degrading." The survey revealed that while there is substantial willingness to assist their bosses and to make his or her job easier, they wish to be treated as co-workers and not as servants. If their working relationship is satisfactory on other counts, getting coffee for the boss is accepted as part of the job.‡

A boss, whether male or female, will find that a secretary, whether male or female, will respond better and achieve more effective results if treated as a professional colleague with valuable skills. Secretaries today are themselves cultivating professional attitudes that are increasingly incorporated in their training programs.

A key principle—respect for the individual—will work for the

*Ibid.
†*The Wall Street Journal*, May 19, 1976, p. 1.
‡Associated Press news release dated December 26, 1974.

benefit of the entire organization. The underutilization of any human resource, male, female, black, or other minority representative, is costly as well as painful to the persons concerned. Each person now in a position of influence in an organization has a unique opportunity to help give real meaning to the concept of "affirmative action."

CHAPTER
10

Wives
and Husbands

Managers, whether male or female, cannot completely divorce their working lives from home and family. A person at work is a total person, the sum of countless demands, responsibilities and role expectations on the part of others. Ideally the manager thrives on a tranquil and supportive outside life as well as on a solid footing within the organization. Realistically, however, the life outside can be as chaotic and frustrating as the life inside.

Many of the skills managers need on the job can carry over into their personal lives. Planning, organizing, decision making, and communicating processes are very much at work. Both husband and wife face the need to protect their personal preferences and private lives against undue inroads by their employing organization or organizations, while at the same time finding a workable accommodation to the expectations of those organizations.

Nonworking Wives

Wives who do not work outside the home, and thus are mainly homemakers, are a vital factor in the success of their husbands. It is seldom possible for the wife of a manager, administrator, or executive to be completely separated from the context of her husband's working or professional life. This is true for several reasons. First, formal and informal social demands confront her to a greater or lesser degree. Second, the organization itself may demand or expect that she play some part in her husband's work activities, such as helping to entertain customers. Third, her husband may need her as a listener, counselor, or sympathetic sounding board by which to judge his actions or make future career plans.

Men differ in the extent and variety of their needs and expectations with respect to their wives. Some have a constant, insatiable need to discuss the day's events each evening. Others are moderate in these expectations; still others are secretive and taciturn. The sensitive wife understands her working husband's needs and expectations, fulfilling them with judgment and good sense. Men, too, should be sensitive to the degree of involvement desired by their wives.

Organizations, too, differ widely in what they expect of their managers' wives. Some insist on a relatively full involvement in formal and social activities; others prefer a selective, moderate degree of involvement; still others have no formal expectations and do not seek to influence the formal or informal participation of wives. In some positions, the role of the wife is genuinely and intrinsically related to the husband's task performance. For example, university presidents or college deans may be expected to do a lot of official entertaining, often of large groups, in their own homes. Moreover, faculty wives tend to form cohesive groups so that the president's wife either formally or informally becomes the "leader" or person of influence among all wives. The higher the level of the wife's husband, the more likely it is that the wife will be drawn into semiofficial obligations of this type.

If the skills and attributes of the wife are important to the organization, it will frequently follow policies of including her in its selection or promotion evaluation procedures. She will be invited to prehiring interviews in which the organization's expectations are indicated. These expectations may include not only participation in appropriate organizational activities but standards of personal conduct as well. She may be expected to become an active citizen in the community through volunteer work, for example. She may come to feel pressures against smoking, drinking, or working outside the home. Some of these pressures are stated in policies; others are subtle and less direct, though nevertheless real.

In all matters pertaining to the manager's nonworking wife, it is important for the wife to understand her own preferences, limitations, and beliefs and to be aware that it is she, not the demanding organization, who makes the decision as to the nature and degree of her involvement in official or social spheres. It is, of course, unethical for an organization to press unwilling wives into activities they dislike or are unable to assume responsibility for. It is also unethical for the organization to penalize a manager whose wife's responses run counter to its expectations. But in a world as it really is, they frequently do act in these unethical ways. It is therefore necessary for a wife to think about the particular situation and her role in it, and then to adhere to the limitations she deems best for herself and her husband. It is a fallacy to believe that the husband cannot be successful and competent unless his wife is totally subservient to the organization's real or imagined needs.

Wives face a particularly difficult problem with respect to the tendency of some organizations to transfer their husbands frequently. The husband's work and career continue; his working contacts and daily life change relatively little in number, scope, and character; his adjustment is quicker and easier. But the wife's social life and the educational and social life of their children undergo more difficult adjustments. The wife may also be cut off from a promising career of her own if she elects to stay with her husband.

Some 40 million persons move each year. Of these, it is estimated that 2.5 million move as the result of corporate transfers. The resulting strains and tensions are traumatic if the cycle of moving and adjustment is repeated too often. Frequent moves dictated by an ambitious husband's career pattern produce personal and marital pressures through their accumulative effects. Offsetting the disadvantages and problems, however, are the benefits of change and the challenge of new opportunities for the entire family. Problems come mainly when moves are too frequent or when they seem to arise out of corporate whim. They occur also when the husband makes a unilateral decision with little or no family discussion.

In matters as important as this, it is wise for the husband who has an opportunity to relocate to discuss it thoroughly with his wife and the children as well. While the transferred husband's role continues and his standing and reputation from the old job accompany him, the wife's and children's ties to the community, social standing, and identities as persons are essentially non-transferable. Their lives become fragmented, disorganized, and temporary through excessive moves. The husband presented with a decision to move can do much to help by being aware of the identity needs of his wife and family. More and more women are highly educated and have wide interests and many skills. Treating them as mere adjuncts or housemaids simply will not suffice in today's world.

It is possible that a disgruntled, unhappy wife not only makes her husband's life difficult but that she also transmits, directly or indirectly, adverse attitudes toward business to their children. The male executive might well ponder his organization's attitude toward the wives of executives. James L. Hayes of the American Management Associations has explained the possible reasons for disgruntled, disaffected corporate wives. A typical corporate attitude is to think of the wife as an adjunct to the husband, sometimes helpful but always a problem. Corporations may analyze the wife's characteristics to see if they match the standards they require, but they seldom give her credit for her contributions. The paycheck goes to the husband alone, though they may have looked at the husband and wife as a team in hiring and promotion decisions. Hayes asserts that companies must modify their approach to see that wives receive more recognition, praise, or even tangible rewards. He suggests such practical policies as paying for wives to travel with their husbands, financing their educational programs, paying for child care, and providing life insurance for wives. The common element in such suggestions is their demonstration that the company recognizes the importance of wives.*

One authority on corporate wives has advised male bosses who work in bleak or dingy surroundings to call on their wives to help

*The Wall Street Journal, January 29, 1975.

them brighten their work environment. In addition to contributing to reduced fatigue and monotony, this is a good way of involving the wife and putting her talents to work.

It is important, however, for the wife to avoid undue interference at her husband's place of work. Some wives are guilty of calling on their husbands at inconvenient, busy times, or of making heavy demands on their husbands' secretaries for mailing out garden club notices and the like. The officious, demanding, jealous or peremptory wife can detract seriously from her husband's effectiveness, just as the considerate, thoughtful wife can be of immense help in his work.

The special need of a non-employed executive wife is to preserve and nourish her own sense of identity and to develop her own important roles. In this process, however, the husband is not merely an innocent bystander. He must understand his wife's role preferences and need for identity. Her roles, and his, both in the home and out of it, are a result of their individual personalities and the character of the relationship they share.

This relationship is not a static one. It changes and grows with time and circumstances. Both wife and husband are active participants in a dynamic process. Each has strengths and capabilities that may enhance or detract from the relationship. It is important for the wife to develop a role that is satisfying for her while at the same time contributing meaningfully to her husband's success.

Through planning and mutually effective communication, husbands and their non-employed wives can arrive at clear understandings about the nature, extent, and significance of the wife's role in organizational affairs. The husband, in particular, must guard against becoming the agent of organizational pressure on the wife. He needs to support her personal differences and decisions. In turn, the wife should, as far as she is able, adapt responses to organizational demands to the nature of her husband's official role and duties.

Employed Wives and Their Husbands

When both husband and wife are pursuing careers or holding jobs, problems similar to those discussed above may occur. There are, however, some additional considerations. First, there are problems of coordination and cooperation. Second, there is the matter of the attitudes and understandings necessary to support dual working careers. Third, there is the impact upon that part of their lives which exists beyond the job and is centered in their home, family, and social life.

Coordination and cooperation become critical factors in the management of dual careers. Schedules and working hours may vary; vacation opportunities may be difficult to bring together; household duties and demands must still be met; transportation problems may arise. These and other procedural, operating problems must be faced. If there are children, additional complexities arise in the coordination and logistics of child care, schooling, running errands, and other activities essential for maintaining each child's identity.

For a working couple, even though their level of cooperation and respect for each other is high, time schedules become extremely important. Work, household chores, and even family fun must be scheduled. There is little time for spontaneous events or for unstructured forms of leisure. The pressure for results is high; unscheduled events are highly disrupting. Fatigue is greater, since both come home from work with housekeeping and other family matters still ahead of them. A wife may have to carry a greater share of the burden, since it is still foreign to the husband's role to engage in more than a minimum of household chores, such as preparing meals, doing laundry, or managing children.

Undoubtedly both husband and wife feel the effect of necessary sacrifices. However, they also enjoy many advantages. The compatibility of dual careers is enhanced when both husband and wife work in the same or similar fields. For example, two physicians or two teachers married to each other may enjoy an enriched extension of their community of personal discourse. There may also be helpful flexibilities in the use of time, the taking of vacations, and the like.

Two special kinds of problems are worth noting. One is the case where one member of the working duality is offered a transfer or promotion elsewhere. The other person has to make a difficult choice between changing jobs or enduring some degree of separation. If one cannot meet the demands or opportunities presented, resentment may develop, as it also might for one who is forced into a change to preserve the marriage.

A second common problem occurs when both husband and wife are working in the same organization. Some organizations maintain policies of not hiring close relatives, at least in the same departments. Others are more flexible about this. In any case, a couple working for the same organization has to guard against situations in which one may appear to exercise favoritism with respect to the other as well as against one's using the other's position for unfair personal advantage.

When husband and wife both work, there may be important status differences in the jobs they hold. If the man has the higher status job, the wife may be perceived as "helping out financially," or "working for the fun of it," or keeping busy to ameliorate the empty-nest syndrome when the children have left home. Fewer problems may ensue, depending upon the image the husband and wife seek to foster, because this situation is much more common than is the reverse. Where the husband has the lower status position, however, adjustment problems are greater. Although this situation is less typical, it is becoming more common because of the progress of women in professional and managerial careers. The wife needs to be aware of the attitudes and feelings of her husband regarding this status differential. The husband, too, must be aware of the greater demands that are being placed upon his wife and must be sensitive to the role that is expected of him.

Routine matters can be rather easily worked out. It is in the areas of psychological and sociological adjustment that the most significant difficulties arise. Attitudes, philosophies, emotions, and life experiences may not readily jibe. One or the other may be more successful or better paid, arousing jealousy or embarrassment. Each may resent the increased need to share undesirable or unfamiliar tasks in the management of home and personal affairs. Communication may be impaired through separations or fatigue. The level of total activity may prevent sufficient listening or deprive one or the other of a needed sounding board. Pressures seem to have fewer outlets and greater adverse effects. Time together is minimized. Disappointments are less readily resolved, emergencies less well handled. Personal relationships may deteriorate from lack of opportunity for reinforcement. Not all these things need occur, but some of them often do.

Fortunately, a working couple can counteract these adverse possibilities by special planning, by keeping communications open, and by mutually supporting and understanding each other. The necessary sacrifices are made to achieve worthwhile goals—greater income and security, use of skills and training, development of individualities and personalities, for example.

Dual careers call not only for planning but also for negotiations. The heart of true negotiation is compromise. Both parties win some and lose some points. Both gain, and both give up things that are important to them. Cooperation, negotiation, and compromise may serve to bring a couple closer together than they might otherwise be, but the pressures may also pull them apart.

Nonworking Husbands

Nonworking husbands, too, may experience the problems of the nonworking wife in reverse, although this situation is less typical. Much depends on the reason for the husband's nonworking status. It may be from illness or from unemployment. Less often, it may be from preference or the circumstance of independent wealth. In today's society, a nonworking male is still an anomaly, perhaps even an embarrassment.

Although social norms in this sphere are changing, an employed wife with a nonworking husband may still need to be sensitive to his feelings of inadequacy, jealousy, or resentment. The successful wife with an unsuccessful or unemployed husband faces special difficulties. It is helpful if the couple can discuss the implications of such a situation and work out mutually satisfactory modes of accommodation.

Planning and Communication

Both husband and wife can gain much from systematic analysis of the nature of the employer or employers' demands on their time and energies. Once made, the analysis becomes the basis for a continuing dialogue about how their work and home responsibilities are affecting them. Where their obligations prove burdensome or difficult, they can jointly plan strategies to improve the situation. With each achieving a better understanding of the other person's responsibilities as well as his or her own, they can minimize the divisive and stressful impacts that often cause strain or tension in a marriage. These processes will also improve job performance through increased confidence in each other and in the ability to respond sensibly to organizational demands and the sharing of the rewards and vicissitudes that always accompany working lives.

The husband and wife can begin by constructing a list of demands and problem areas for which they will need to have policies or make decisions. Typical items on this list for the husband are:

☐ Skill, knowledge, and technical demands
☐ Regularly scheduled hours of effort in specific locations
☐ Extra duty requirements beyond regularly scheduled hours, bringing work home, community involvement, meeting business contacts
☐ The need to commute to and from work and methods of doing so
☐ Social requirements, such as office parties, golf outings, travel to conventions, and entertaining customers
☐ Level of effort and required difficulty of the work, requirements for advancement
☐ The nature and extent of friendships to be encouraged among colleagues, superiors, and subordinates
☐ The husband's relationship to home, wife, and children

Typical items on the wife's list are:

☐ Kinds of occasions on which she is expected to participate in social functions or business activities, travel requirements
☐ Degree of visibility expected of her as an executive's wife
☐ Expectations regarding visits to the office, telephone calls, and the like
☐ Extent to which the organization believes that the wife contributes substantially to the husband's success

☐ The wife's responsibility for helping the children understand
their father's work and adjustment to the organization's activities and demands
☐ The development of desirable, acceptable outlets to enhance
her own identity and encourage personal growth

   Each list should be concise but contain enough detail to facili-
tate the second step: a discussion of the priorities of the items
on each list. For example, if the wife was interviewed by
someone in the organization at the time her husband was interviewed, she knows that the organization has an interest in her as
a wife. From the nature of the interview she can ascertain some
of the organization's expectations as to the extent of involvement
for the wives of its members. Similarly the husband may evaluate
the social, political, and technical demands upon him. From
analyzing these lists, each can develop a profile of the essential
points of separate and mutual involvement in the organization.
   Working on these lists can provide a number of benefits for the
wife and husband. First, each learns more about what is expected
of the other. Second, clarifications can result from the process of
discussing the items and writing them down. Third, you have the
information upon which to base decisions regarding your own
preferences to solve some of the problems you may have in developing your preferred role in relation to the organization.

Widowhood

The man of the house, if he is the family breadwinner, has special
responsibilities for estate planning and for teaching his wife how
to manage family and personal matters if he dies before she does.
The wife has a responsibility to consider her role and skills as
well. Most wives survive on lower incomes than the couple
shares. A study of 1,744 urban widows, for example, showed that
the family with an income of over $15,000 lost an average of 57
percent of that income in the first two years after the husband's
death. Taxes, wills, insurance, company benefits, pensions, and
investments call for a searching examination and mutual exploration.*

*Alfred Allen Lewis, with Barrie Burns, *Three Out of Four Wives* (New York:
Macmillan, 1975).

The odds now are that at the age of 70, one of every two women will be a widow. Two-thirds of the women in the United States die as widows, and the average duration of widowhood is nine years. One reason for this is biological: women have longer life expectancies. A second reason is sociocultural—men tend to marry younger women. Occupations show interesting variations in their mortality rates. Poorly paid occupations have the shortest life expectancies, as do bartenders, physicians, U.S. Senators, and U.S. Presidents. Male executives, contrary to widespread opinion, have the lowest mortality rates of any group, and the higher the executive's position, the lower the mortality rate.

Although the feminist movement may be creating more independent, self-reliant women able to cope with a variety of problems, the more typical situation is that women are not brought up in our society to act independently, especially in financial matters. Our culture does not adequately prepare women for living alone. Thus a husband should consider how he may help his wife cope with the eventuality of widowhood.

Developing Roles Creatively

Managers, whether men or women, can creatively approach external problems as well as on-the-job matters. Their respective roles are only in part determined by society or by the organizations for which they work. There is ample room for the elaboration of work and family roles that reflect the full range of needs of husbands, wives and children. Since people and organizations experience continuous change, husbands and wives should continuously review and modify their role responses.

A story, probably apocryphal, is told that years ago on the eastern edge of the great prairies a sign was erected to warn travelers: "Choose your rut carefully. You will be in it for the next 500 miles." Clearly your choices as a manager represent commitments that are not easy to change or abandon.

Your own sense of accomplishment and achievement is vital. You are probably more knowledgeable than others about your strengths and weaknesses and the degree of your effectiveness. Recognition of your achievements by others is also important, even essential. Without reinforcing feedback from others you are deprived of learning opportunities and a basis for objective evaluation. You have a right to be proud of the results of your efforts and to expect the rewards to be commensurate.

One final prescription: have fun. One large corporation listed seven objectives for 1975. The first six were standard: serve our customers, make a profit, and so on. The final one was "to have fun." In a world of tribulation and much ground for pessimism, this may be the most difficult of all the objectives to attain. But one who attains it is fortunate indeed.

CHAPTER
11

Staying on Top of Your Work

Competent executive and managerial talent is one of the scarcest commodities in today's complex organizations. Developed talents become obsolete due to rapid change. Complexities of organizational life seem ever more exasperating. The manager's task thus becomes more demanding and, all too often, excessively frustrating. Successful managers develop the habit of controlling their work and their jobs so as to stay ahead of the game. They cope with a myriad of difficult problems without unduly succumbing to pressures that seek to destroy their effectiveness.

In the context of modern organizations, the vital, adventurous, and risk-taking spirit energizes the creative manager. The manager's world is one of action as well as of analysis, and the action-oriented manager has the best chance of surmounting the obstacles that abound. We may agree with Lloyd George that "the finest eloquence is that which gets things done."

"Management," one authority suggests, "is what happens in the white spaces outside the boxes of the organization charts." This comment recognizes what many managers realize intuitively—that the traditional, pyramidal bureaucracy has never been the tight system it was thought to be. Harlan Cleveland has argued that pyramidal systems must give way to organizational models in which control is loose, power is diffused, and centers of decision are widespread. Though there are powerful and compelling forces that tend to strengthen the manager's domain consciousness, there are increasing pressures moving organizational systems to flatter structures, greater use of informal or temporary arrangements, and more flexible, consultative, and adaptive managerial styles. There can be no question that today's managers find their tasks harder and their jobs tougher than those required by the traditional bureaucratic model.*

Many managers, however, still have to swim upstream against the routinizing and leveling tendencies of the bureaucracy. They have to resist compartmentalization and the restrictions of stereotyped roles. They have been trained and provided with experience mainly in organizations relying largely on bureaucratic precepts. Survival of the individual and of the organization remain strong instincts in the bureaucratically trained psyche. Nevertheless, staying on top of one's job as a manager means looking toward the future and learning to use new concepts, new tools, and new styles of management practice.

Workaholism

The pressure of hard work impinges heavily on managers. Hard work in itself is not bad. If meaningful, productive, and balanced by periods of rest and relaxation, work does not harm the manager who is physically fit. However, continuous hard work in the form of relentless, unremitting effort born of slavish adherence to habit or excessive subservience to tasks or a boss is known as workaholism.

The manifestations of workaholism are found in the individual's failure to take vacations; the bulging briefcase carried home each night; the desk piled high with reports, documents for clearance, and voluminous paperwork. Workaholics never get caught up with their work. They have records of postponed, canceled, or missed appointments. They are late for meetings. Haste and fatigue are evident, as are the workaholic's fanatical pleasure and pride in staying on the job all day and half the night.

The workaholic is a work addict—a manager whose work behavior is compulsive. Such a person simply cannot take time off.

---

* Harlan Cleveland, *The Future Executive* (New York: Harper & Row, Publishers, Inc., 1972).

Separation from the office is painful When away, the workaholic uses the telephone constantly to keep in close touch with infinite details back home. Workaholics are unable to relax, take vacations, or enjoy the fun and games that enliven the days of the more relaxed people in the organization.

Workaholics get credit for hard work, but their achievements may be at extreme personal cost to themselves, to their families, or even to the organization itself. Workaholism may develop as a protective device to shield the individual from home, family or other outside responsibilities. It may also represent an extreme sense of devotion or commitment to a boss, an organization, or to a professional field. Some workaholism is inherent in the technical requirements of work, as in the case of farming where the farmer works, seasonally at least, from early dawn to late at night. Small, independent businessmen may work a 60- to 80-hour week. Workaholics tend to be found principally in the professions, in managerial ranks, and among the self-employed. Some workaholism occurs through imitation of, or coercion by, a boss. One company president, for example, regularly telephones his managers' offices at 8 or 9 P.M. If they don't answer, he deems them "domestically oriented," and their careers are truncated.

Workaholism is accompanied by substantial physical stress and mental tension. Ulcers and other physical ailments occur frequently in this group. Workaholics are not simply people who work hard, they work hard to the point where they suffer severe pain, trauma, or other symptoms when deprived of work. They suffer anxiety, depression, or both. They are escaping, through work, other responsibilities that cause them pain. Physical as well as mental breakdown may accompany prolonged workaholism.

Workaholics are suffering persons with complex psychological problems whose origins lie deep in their personalities and backgrounds. They need professional help from competent counselors and psychologists. Organizations should not ignore workaholics, and their colleagues and bosses should assist them in seeking treatment. They need the understanding of those around them.

Workaholics resent other workaholics who reform themselves. It is acceptable to complain about "the rat race," but not to abandon it. It is hard not to be a workaholic in an organization that is full of them, especially at the top. To the extent that the workaholism is organizationally fostered, a change of employers may be indicated. Hard work, then, short of workaholism, is part of the success strategy of the creative manager. The truly able person knows his own limitations and can keep his levels of effort within practicable bounds. A balanced flow of energy directed alternately at tough, demanding tasks and periods of relative relaxation is a key resource for the creative manager.

Making the Most of Your Time

Your time is one of your most fundamental assets. It should be guarded carefully, without denying it to those who have a meaningful need for it. There should be a clock in your office plainly visible to visitors. One vice-president rather dramatically used an alarm clock. Those seeking appointments were required to ask for a definite amount of time. Often the vice-president would negotiate with the prospective caller. The alarm was set to allow the agreed-upon time, and the bell signaled visitors to leave. Some resented this stratagem; others scoffed. But it did force a more effective use of time both for the vice-president and for the persons who called on him.

Time-efficient executives all too often save their own time at the cost of the time of others. For example, some managers restrict phone calls or visiting hours to a certain period of the day. If not carefully watched, this reduction in availability can add to the time burdens of those who find their work delayed until the manager can be reached. In saving time you need to be aware of the total effect of your strategies on other people in the organization, for their time is valuable too. Moreover, your approach provides a model which, through emulation, will help others throughout the organization.

An essential ingredient of time management is an analysis of the basic kinds of demands on one's time. A plan of time management can then be constructed around the demand analysis. This plan becomes a general habit pattern, but it need not be a rigid, inflexible set of routines. The time management plan is a set of guidelines and personal policies which, when it becomes known to others, teaches them appropriate ways and times for managing their interventions on your time.

The main categories in the time management plan are (1) personal outside time, (2) personal inside time for meditation, reflection, and creative innovative thinking, (3) time for day-to-day operating problems in functional responsibilities, and (4) time for clients, subordinates, colleagues, and other people with appropriate claims on time.

Day-to-day operating problems are great thieves of time. They encroach on planned time distributions because of their immediate urgency. No one escapes his share of crisis managing or "putting out fires." With careful planning, however, the creative manager can minimize these unscheduled demands. Each manager should also review the definition of what constitutes a genuine crisis or operating problem, and who must handle it. It is surprising how ordinary happenings are declared to be crises simply because the declarers know they can get immediate action from the managers who pride themselves on handling emergencies. Many so-called crises will fade or will be handled by subordinates who rise to the occasion if a reasonable period of time is allowed to elapse. The persistent crisis-seeker is often a poor delegator or a crisis creator.

By sorting out the crisis events into their realities and urgencies, the creative manager saves time and involves others in the problem. In the same way, a manager needs to control requests for personal contact from persons inside and outside his organization. Here one's skill in appointment management counts heavily, and a good secretary who can tactfully screen people is a priceless gem. One executive, for example, in examining his time analysis, saw that he spent nearly 20 percent of his time seeing people who had no real need to see him. It had been necessary to refer them to others for action. While there may be value in accessibility, hand holding, and public relations effects in a "see anyone" policy, these benefits have to be compared with the total time problem and the manager's relative priorities of activity. People usually try to see someone as high in an organization as they can, even when someone at a lower level could be more helpful. This "shoot high" syndrome represents a serious en-croachment upon managerial time.

Personal, outside time is an important category. Even short of workaholism, today's busy manager faces heavy demands for meetings, travel, and civic duties that lead to neglect of family and personal development. The job mix should be analyzed to assess the genuine need for the use of off-hours time.

The need for outside activity is related to the problem of time for reflection and meditation. The creative manager needs time to be alone, to think and plan, to read broadly beyond trade or professional literature. Many managers have found the tenets of transcendental meditation of great value: a few minutes or even an hour a day set aside for letting thoughts come and go, and for ruminating about life in general.

How to Save Time Without Really Bothering Anyone

The executive's daily workload consists of a unique mixture of events. These events are usually reflected in prosaic terms, such as phone calls, requests or messages from clerical and secretarial personnel, letters, and audiences with visitors. Efficiency and good morale of the work group are increased when the executive handles these matters with dispatch. Delay in answering mail, or unavailability for phone calls, meetings, or talking with visitors, makes it difficult for other people to get their work done. Although delays of one kind or another can sometimes produce strategic benefits to the executive or the organization, this device can be used to excess and can produce exorbitant costs in time, money, or the executive's reputation for difficult dealing.

It is helpful for the executive to deliberate at some length on the management of internal office affairs. Time is among the most precious of resources, and the distribution of one's own time is a most imperative management skill. There is strategic value in projecting an image of extreme busyness; yet this can be over-done. However, the executive cannot afford to grant all claims against his time. The executive whose time is valuable and who realizes that it is will find that others place a commensurate value upon it and will tend to show greater consideration when making their demands.

The beginning point in managing time is to draw up a weekly time budget. Starting with commitments that are more or less firm, such as regular staff meetings, periodic conferences, or other routine commitments, the time budget can be constructed so as to contain time plans for reading mail, dictating correspondence, or visiting outside locations. Once these basic considerations are built in, the executive can develop with his secretary a subsidiary plan for the handling of phone calls and visitors.

For handling the telephone, the executive can instruct his secretary to hold his calls so that several may be answered during one 30-minute period. For visitors, the executive usually needs a planned system of appointments. Casual visiting can be discouraged. As others get to know the executive's work patterns, they adjust to the habits he manifests.

As an aid to establishing a time plan, the manager should make careful records for a typical week or month showing exactly how he is spending his time. These records can then be studied to spot ways in which time management can be improved. Peter Drucker has provided a useful concept: discretionary time, the period in which the manager exercises a choice over what he is doing. The other part of his time is that which must be allocated to others or over which the manager is subject to the initiatives of others. The aim of this part of the analysis is to protect and even enlarge the discretionary time sector.

Time management experts list the following preventable time-wasters:

1. Spending too much time on problems brought by subordinates.
2. Oversupervising subordinates.
3. Undersupervising subordinates, thus fostering consequent crises.
4. Scheduling less important work before more important (and possibly more unattractive) work.
5. Starting a job before thinking it through.
6. Leaving jobs before completion.
7. Doing things that can be delegated to another person, such as a secretary.
8. Doing things that can be delegated to modern equipment.

9. Doing things that actually aren't a part of your real job.
10. Spending too much time on your previous area of interest or competence.
11. Doing unproductive things from sheer habit.
12. Keeping too many, too complicated, or overlapping records.
13. Pursuing projects that one probably can't achieve.
14. Paying too much attention to low-yield projects.
15. Failing to anticipate crises.
16. Handling too wide a variety of duties.
17. Shrinking from new or unfamiliar duties.
18. Failing to build barriers against interruptions.
19. Allowing conferences and discussions to wander after their purpose is fulfilled.
20. Conducting unnecessary meetings, visits, and phone calls.
21. Chasing trivial data after the main facts are in.ˋ
22. Engaging in personal work or conversations before starting business work.
23. Socializing at great length between tasks.
24. Failing to analyze one's own use of time.
25. Letting paperwork become a "security blanket."
26. Working on petty details first and saving the big tasks for later.

Here are eight time stretchers:

1. Using the telephone to save time-consuming writing effort, but avoiding needless waste of time by idle telephoning.
2. Starting the day with a list of key things to do, then doing them, noting the items that stay on the list rather than getting accomplished.
3. Learning to skim reports, reading summaries and digests, and demanding conciseness from others.
4. Being selective in reading journals, magazines, and trade reports.
5. Learning how to use idle time, even if brief moments, for some worthy purpose.
6. Looking for repetitive tasks that can be delegated or bunched together to save time.

7. Studying the overall pattern of the workday for possible redistribution of effort for maximum accomplishment.
8. Blocking out the best, most quiet hours for concentrating on your most important, creative work.

Merely being aware of the various time leaks that intrude upon one's work is not enough. It requires substantial personal discipline to make the hard decisions that guard one's time. Excessive planning and control of time could close off opportunities for learning, for capitalizing on momentary, unexpected events, or for the enjoyment of flexibility and change. On balance, the executive needs to steer a steady, knowledgeable course between rigid control and relaxed flexibility. Self-perception is helpful. If an executive knows the dangers of the erosion of his most valuable time and that use of time reflects his fears, worries, and tensions as well as his enjoyment of fun and games, he is well on his way toward avoiding a slavish, mechanistic domination by the clock.

Working Conditions and Meetings

The environment in which you do your important thinking is an important consideration. Your office should be a quiet one, comfortably and completely, though not necessarily lavishly, furnished. The decor should be one of your own choosing, depending on your personality, work habits, and interests. You should be able to choose wall paintings and other decorations.

From time to time a manager needs a change of pace. Sometimes this is done by scheduling meetings and conferences in a fresh, out-of-the-office environment. In a new environment, tough problems can often be seen more clearly and insights come to mind that are not possible in a habitual environment.

The idea of a retreat appeals to many executives with thinking and planning responsibilities. This entails a visit to a selected quiet resort environment away from urban congestion. A location that gets you back to nature is good. Reflection, relaxation, and thought go together in retreat settings.

You can go on a retreat by yourself or with a carefully selected working group. The advantage is to get away from the telephone and from the intrusion of people into your discretionary time. Another advantage is the possibility of cross-fertilization of ideas. A relatively open agenda in the work session brings out ideas. Brainstorming is in order.

Alternating working and planning sessions are beneficial, such as a pattern of working intensively in the morning and relaxing in the afternoon. One executive has said, "Freeing myself physically in tennis or golf after an intense work session helps me to achieve greater mental freedom. Being forced to shelve a knotty problem while I play golf is a relief, and when I come back to the work session, I often find insights I wasn't looking for. It allows me to tap fresh wells of thought."

The creative manager knows how to conduct himself at a conference table as well as in less formal meeting situations. The fruitfulness of meetings depends heavily on the attitudes of the persons present. For example, are they aware of the purpose of the meeting? Are they in sympathy with the meeting? What might be gained or lost? Who is trying to prove what? Who wants to persuade anyone of anything? Are the participants merely there because they have to be? Are they on the defensive or offensive?

Meetings provide an excellent context in which to develop your listening skills. Many words are exchanged in face-to-face meetings. It is necessary to focus on latent, derivative meanings to get beneath the surface of things. Warm-up talk, for example, may ease the group into its hard work but have little substantive value. Winding-up talk, too, fulfills key functions, such as setting minds to rest, restoring the confidence of winners and losers, and providing a feeling of closure. But these are not central aims.

There are always two agendas: the manifest, or stated, agenda and the hidden agenda. The hidden agenda is often the real action center of the meeting. Separate meetings cannot practicably be called for the myriad of purposes people have in mind. Hence they will bring up their problems whenever they have the opportunity to. The executive who chairs a meeting typically wants to be open, democratic, and flexible, yet he cannot allow hidden agendas to crowd out the original purposes.

Often a disproportionate amount of time will go to the hidden or informal agenda item. For example, one committee had to make a million-dollar decision on land acquisition. Someone brought up the matter of coffee dispensers. Result: an hour on coffee dispensing and a left-over ten minutes on the land decisions.

Hidden agendas are inevitable and should probably not be eliminated. If people are excited or emotionally involved, it is best not to shut off the flow of communication unless it too seriously distorts or aborts the main purposes. The hidden agenda emerges gradually and can be seen only by the careful observer. It may or may not be a suitable use of the group's time.

Meetings run better if persons attending them really do their homework. They can plan and prepare only if they know the purposes and agenda in advance. They should also know who is attending, how long the meeting is expected to last, and what will be expected of them. It is a good thing to start a meeting promptly, and to end it at a reasonable, even preplanned, time. Most meetings can be shorter than they turn out to be. An hour is maximum for most meetings.

Effectiveness and Self-Knowledge

Effectiveness, like success, is a habit. Every executive or manager quite literally holds down two jobs: the one he is doing and the greater one he aspires to do and is capable of doing. The best work is done by those who think about something more than the confines of their jobs and what they are, rather than what they could be.

An undue concern about security can impede effectiveness, for the antithesis of security is change and growth. Most managers find it possible to feel secure when they are in the right job, are competent to do what they are doing, and have achieved a degree of self-understanding. One has to like oneself well enough to be proud of his education, his experience, his accomplishments. The manager who hasn't developed self-respect will probably not get it from others.

One mark of an effective executive is found in the development of other people. This means delegating, monitoring, coaching, and appraising subordinates and allowing them to take risks. A primary task is to develop one's successor. This has to be done without overemphasizing the contemplated successor as a "fair-haired boy."

There is a difference between effectiveness and efficiency. Efficiency is a cost-benefit concept—getting the most at the least cost. Effectiveness is the ability to find the right jobs and to get them done in the world of creative action. Efficiency is highly desirable, but exaggerated emphasis on it may abort effectiveness by diluting creativity and spontaneity. Bureaucratic routines and restrictions are often justified in the name of efficiency at the expense of effectiveness. This does not mean that bureaucratic concepts are to be stamped out, but rather that they should be wisely used, leaving room for variations, flexibilities, and departures from the norm.

Self-appraisal for most is more difficult than appraising others, yet a person who knows how well he is doing is likely to continue to do better. Realistic self-criticism, though difficult, breeds honesty in one's personal relationships.

Each individual has his personal unique set of weaknesses and strengths. It is important to be aware of them, along with their consequences, and through such awareness, to develop a balanced managerial style. Some psychologists have found that a given trait can be simultaneously both a weakness and a strength. For example, a vice-president may be admired for boldness and vigor, yet people may also feel that he is too impulsive. Or a person may be appreciated for being careful and methodical, but some might wonder why he hesitates so long to take action. Thus a person's weaknesses are often an overextension of strengths. The strength and the weakness are attached to the same behavior. This leads to the major idea that a manager does not have a single, unvarying managerial style but rather adapts his style to different situations and contexts.

Knowing the strong-weak dimensions of your style repertoire can help you capitalize on your strengths, giving you momentum in areas where your strengths are particularly useful. You can also develop the support of others to help you compensate for your weaknesses by picking the right subordinates or choosing the colleagues with whom you work. A helpful strategy is to find opportunities to work in the same areas in which you are weakest, to acquire experience and test your capabilities. Finally, where weaknesses are the result of overextensions of strengths, you should guard against such overextensions by controlling and directing their use. There is evidence that the effectiveness dimension of management style changes as one rises to the top. In the beginning levels, tasks are more specific, more specialized, more routinized, and more readily evaluated. In higher positions, these qualities are less evident and are replaced by the need for the generalist, the communicator, the interpreter, the coordinator, the outside rather than the inside person. The need for an aggressive "do it" style gives way to the need for a "coaching" style. Thus the advancing manager's career goes through several stages of transition. If these stages remain unrecognized, the trauma and strain become severe, since the individual holds responsibilities to which he has not adjusted.

Mental and Physical Health

Coping with trauma, strain, and tension is a necessary skill to develop. Failure to do so damages both mental and physical health. Predisposition to certain states of health is part of our genetic heritages, but living habits are important determinants of an individual's health status. Health, energy, and alertness are essential for the effective, creative executive.

Some organizations are neutral or even indifferent to problems of health. Though considerable attention to the health and safety of employees is required by federal legislation, the laws are complex and sometimes unclear. By contrast, other organizations have extensive policies on the matters of health. Some insist on and pay for annual physical examinations for executives.

The creative manager guards his health. Personal health habits, such as eating properly, getting plenty of sleep, providing for relaxation, and proper exercise are fundamental.

One of the main causes of breakdowns in health is excessive stress and tension within the person and within the work situation.

Personal stress can injure the health of successful people. Indeed, moving up the ladder of success increases the strain and tension. In one case, an executive had been working 17 hours a day. He demanded perfection in himself and in others for he was moving up the ladder fast. Then the man started to have dizzy and fainting spells for which doctors could find no physical disorder. One day in a meeting while he was listening to a presentation, he took a box of kitchen matches out of his brief case and piled them high on the table in front of him. Just as the speaker was reaching his main point, he lit the pile of matches. He eventually received professional therapy.

Situationally induced stress is also an important cause of trouble. Sooner or later, every manager reaches a level in the organization where danger signals need to be heeded. The pace of modern organization is often fast and unrelenting. If one recognizes danger signals in time, situational factors can be avoided or corrected. One may seek a change in the organization or a new job somewhere else. The creative manager keeps practicing the skills of delegation, time-saving, and relaxation to relieve situational stresses.

A cardiologist has described three types of persons according to their response to stress: first there are the "iron men," those who accept heavy loads with a smile and little outward sign of pressure. Then there are the "glass men" for whom the same heavy load is borne with a calm exterior but who may crack under the strain. Finally, there are the "rubber men" who are malleable, beaten by circumstances, sagging with their burdens.

Our cavemen ancestors used up excess adrenaline in the fight for survival or to escape from enemies. But for modern man, adrenaline is detrimental, for there is no immediate release for it. This results in high blood pressure, the No. 1 cause of heart failure, kidney failure, and strokes. In the United States, an estimated 27 million people suffer from high blood pressure. Half of them don't even know they have it. And of those who do know they have it, half are not being properly treated.

To relieve stress, the creative manager keeps things in perspective by asking what's important—the job, prestige, social standing, or family? Creative managers also learn to pace themselves. Few managers can stay in the "iron man" category indefinitely.

Fear of the unknown in newer jobs of higher responsibility frequently contributes to feelings of stress and tension. The work ethic in American society implacably adds to the pressure. Unless one is a success, others look down upon him. People rising to high positions often seem to feel the need to appear omnipotent, to do everything themselves, and to know more than anyone else on the job.

Since one's self-concept has a great deal to do with how one performs, each person should put himself through a process of self-appraisal to find out who he is and what he is all about. It helps him to cope with strengths and weaknesses. It helps him to be realistic in his outlook. One authority has said, "When you know who you are and what your expectations are, your prospects are fantastic. You are no longer working for the company or an organization, you are working for your own true self. Only then can you begin to grow."

A severe health problem for managers and executives is alcoholism. An estimated 10 percent of all employees, including managers and executives, are alcoholics. Alcoholism is a complex problem of deep interest to managers, social workers, medical personnel, and researchers. Nevertheless, it is not clear what the causes or cures may be. The costs, however, are very high to the organization, to the individual, and to his family. One of the fundamental ideas governing work on alcoholism is that it is a disease, not a moral or legal matter entirely.

The business world was recently shocked by a retired automobile executive who claimed that he had to drink his way up the corporate ladder. He filed a $1.3 million suit against the firm, accusing it of turning him into an alcoholic. The executive who filed suit had progressed up the ladder to a $60,000-a-year position in the international sector of the firm's operation during a 26-year period. He was asked in 1971 to sign a letter of resignation. He claimed that the company broke oral and written employment contracts by not helping him overcome the drinking problem. After his resignation, his wife and children left, and he lost his $70,000 dream house. He could no longer hold a job, completely losing interest in work. In 1972, he stopped drinking after a 17-day alcoholic treatment program. He was later reunited with his family and embarked again on a successful job. This case history reveals much of the misery and conflict connected with cases of alcoholism.

Excessive weight is a health factor of widespread importance to managers. Being overweight invites high blood pressure, diabetes, and other serious problems. Mayor Orville L. Hubbard of Dearborn, Michigan in 1974 put city officials on a crash diet. "Fat guys don't do much," he said. "You have to lose weight if you want to work here," was his dictum. He gave them a deadline for trimming down from two to ten pounds each. Hubbard, who weighed 238 pounds himself, set an even tougher goal for himself. "If I'm alive on December 31, 1974, I will be 75 pounds lighter than I am today," he vowed. While it is doubtful that administrative fiats can always be successful, some degree of recognition of the problem by administrators is an important step forward.

One survey by an employment agency in 1974 covering 15,000 executives placed by the agency showed that fat people are paid less than thin people. "Some people are paying a penalty of as much as $1,000 per pound," said the president of the agency. "The overweight has become America's largest, least protected minority group," he declared. Fat people, he said, suffer from the image of being slow, sloppy, inefficient, and lacking self-control. However, he also said that in 25 years of experience he found these myths to be completely false. Unfortunately, he added, the overweight generally make less money than their slimmer counterparts, are less likely to be hired for top spots, and are more likely to be ignored when promotion time arrives.

The agency selected at random 1,000 people who had been placed by major branch offices in their firm. Their measurements were compared with insurance industry charts showing normal weights for people of various heights and ages. Individuals who weighed at least 10 percent more than their normal weight, according to the charts, were considered overweight. Of 1,500 executives who earned top salaries of $25,000 to $50,000 only 9 percent were overweight. But of the 13,500 who earned in the $10,000 to $20,000 range, 30 percent were more than 10 pounds overweight.

One of the strategies important to the executive who seeks to preserve his health is to have an annual physical examination. Some are reluctant to take the time and spend the money for an annual physical. The annual physical is controversial even among doctors, some of whom do not like to see well people. However, a precautionary school of thought holds that the annual physical can be an important preventive measure because it often uncovers latent or hidden disease and other defects. Many firms pay for regular annual physicals on the part of their key executives.

Aging

Everyone is subject to the aging process, but in various ways, each resists recognizing this fact. In the United States in recent years, youth is revered more than age. Organizations differ in their treatment of the aging manager and in their policies for meeting the needs of aging employees. Yet on the positive side, many are conducting pre-retirement planning programs and developing more adequate pensions and other benefits. Uniform mandatory retirement ages are widespread, but plans for keeping employees beyond the nominal retirement age by shifting them to other work are more numerous. The maturing executive who makes appropriate plans for each stage of his career, including retirement, is prepared to accept and adapt to the aging process.

A major study has found that old age does not bring great changes in capability and life style. Presumably there are shifts of interest and declining energy patterns, but mental competence levels out and is reinforced by the accumulation of wisdom and experience. Old age tends to continue the habits and capabilities launched in the earlier years of one's life. The researchers found that the people they studied became more complex, distinctive personalities rather than losing individuality with age.

The youthful manager may well consider that some day others will perceive him as being old and subject him to prejudiced, stereotyped attitudes they hold toward the aged. The older manager may well benefit from a respect for youth rather than jealousy or cynicism. The older manager and the retired person need, much as younger persons do, a wide variety of options and possibilities open to them, without the artificial barriers of age classification or stereotyped thinking. Individuality is what counts for aging persons, both in their own attitudes and in the attitudes of others toward them.

The aging manager is in good company. During the next 15

years, the 30–45 age group will increase from 36.5 million to about 60 million, and the 65-and-over group will increase from 22 million to about 30 million. The other age groups will grow significantly, and the school age groups will decline. Thus the labor market will be short on youth and long on maturity. It is a waste of human resources to ignore the possibilities of the near-and-over-65 age group as a source of experienced, stable, and dedicated workers.

Courage

It takes courage to find and tackle the tougher tasks which add up to being a more effective manager. It is easy to cultivate the appearance of effectiveness by sticking to comfortable routines. To venture, to take risks, to try the difficult or the impossible, is the mark of an exceptional person.

In 1976 Phillipe Petit, a French aerialist, exemplified courage by walking 1,350 feet above ground on a tightrope stretched between the twin towers of the World Trade Center in New York City. "If I see two towers," he said later, "I have to walk." It takes courage to see and accept such a challenge.

The opportunities in organizational life may not seem as dramatic or as likely to achieve public acclaim. But the challenges are nevertheless abundant and real. Physical courage is not the issue. Rather it is a mental, philosophical, professional, or spiritual courage that is needed. It is the courage to define what is the right thing to do and to do it. Often this requires following an unpopular course against strong disapproval or opposition. It reflects the loneliness of true leadership. Courage is not recklessness or bravado or the pursuing of opponents at all costs. It is a subtle, quiet, patient process reflecting one's confidence in oneself and others.

CHAPTER
12

Learning to Live
with Your Job

Job holding is an art more taken for granted than cultivated as one of life's useful skills. One either has or does not have a job. To think seriously about one's position in the world of work requires a rather special point of view that may at first seem unfamiliar. This point of view is best described as a professional outlook. Any manager can develop professional attitudes that lead to a useful and satisfying lifetime work experience. But developing professional attitudes requires careful introspection and self-analysis.

Merely holding a job by routinely fulfilling its minimum requirements does not enhance your job satisfaction. It may or may not satisfy your boss. When an organization restricts by design or otherwise the self-fulfilling tendencies in people, employees are forced to compartmentalize their lives into outside and inside sectors. The inside sector is tolerated to maximize returns from the outside sector. The outside is where many managers do their real living.

For at least two generations now we have known a fact which argues against such compartmentalization. Every individual is a unique and complete self that cannot be divided without unsatisfactory consequences both for the individual and his organization.

Unless we blame only the organization, managers have to learn how to achieve fulfillment in their jobs. There is a shared responsibility for mutual satisfaction between working men and women and their organizations. Therefore, creative managers examine how they approach their jobs to see whether they are really living with them (and through them), or whether they are merely tolerating a mundane existence.

This is where professional attitudes call for scrutiny. The first thing to do is to ignore the traditional concept of a professional person as a member of an elite group enjoying special preferences in society. Studies of prestige rankings reveal the high social status of professional occupations such as medicine, law, teaching, and the ministry. Lesser occupations seek to emulate the conditions which confer this high social standing and thereby to help practitioners achieve security, autonomy, and higher incomes.

Such strivings are dead-end aspirations in management. They are a superficial and hollow mockery of the forces which bring out the best in each person. The mechanical apparatus of the traditional professions—licensing, controlled access, fees for service, and self-protective codes—are impractical for managers. But even in the traditional professions, such requirements are often more honored in the breach than in the daily events of work experience. The only standard requirement of the professions available to managers is that for specialized education and training through practical experience.

Managerial Attitudes

Professional attitudes, however, are not the exclusive property of an elite. Managers cannot become an elite group by adopting the trappings of professionalism, but the attitudes of the professional are available to anyone regardless of salary, level of position, or type of work. Let us explore and illustrate just the most important of these attitudes.

THE MATTER OF ETHICS

This is one of the most fundamental attitudes of the professional person. Most people tend to think of themselves as generally ethical in their conduct. They favor ethical behavior in principle but recognize that human foibles and pecadilloes will occasionally creep in. One of the toughest problems is the insidious nature of social pressures within a group that replace ethical norms with expediencies and the belief that any means is justified for a worthwhile end. This is exactly the problem pervading the Watergate scandals. Here we saw well-established professionals with law degrees and master's degrees in business and economics sacrificing the principles inherent in their educations to further the selfish interests of a coterie of public power grabbers. Clearly there is little necessary connection between being educated and being ethical. Much of our worst ethical behavior emanates from well-educated elites.

THE MATTER OF COMPETENCE

Professional persons generally have a high need for achievement. They take pride in both the complexities and the simplest details of their work. Professionals try to keep up with changing knowledge in their fields. They are learning all the time, which makes them inquisitive and analytical. When things go wrong they want to know why. They constantly hope for new opportunities to apply their skills and knowledge in better ways.

In modern organizations, the old stereotype of an authoritarian boss and a "do-as-you-are-told" subordinate is passing. Such a mold forces the subordinate into conformist, subservient, and immature attitudes. It results in defensive, devious, and self-protective behavior. Much better is the idea that boss and subordinate form a working team. The operating principle of the team approach is that each learns from the other, and each teaches the other. This idea recognizes that faultfinding and overbearing attitudes interfere with an objective analysis of problems, distort the communication process, and lead to a lack of trust which aborts effective behavior.

Studs Terkel, in his book *Working*, came up with gloomy findings about the meaning of work to individuals in many fields.* From several hundred interviews among all types of workers, he concludes that almost all working people utterly dislike their jobs and occupations. They hate their employers, and they hate the pressures and the circumstances which enslave

*New York: Pantheon, 1964.

them. If this picture is fairly drawn, it is a serious indictment of our management skills. Yet I believe that Terkel somehow missed interviewing many who have not let adverse circumstances deflect them from living fulfilled working lives.

Technical and professional competence is one of the main keys to living with your job. Competence can be practiced, learned, maintained, and directed for your benefit and that of your organization. It is one of the most valid assurances that a good job will be yours, and that you will occupy a challenging place in a successful organization.

The person who has both competence and a sense of ethical conduct is a standout. Such persons will be noticed and rewarded because they are scarce in today's marketplace.

THE HIGH PRIORITY GIVEN TO SERVING OTHERS

This point of view places professional service ahead of selfish gain. It collides with the common stereotype of individuals as essentially acquisitive, selfish persons. The stereotype is not true. Some individuals are perhaps innately selfish and acquisitive; others may learn to be this way when the organization rewards such behavior or when more positive behaviors go unrecognized or unrewarded. Most people will respond effectively when they are linked together as a team with challenges to meet.

It is not always easy to place service high on one's list of priorities. We can say that service yields its own reward through pride of accomplishment. We can say that reward usually follows the skillful performance of one's job. But where these results do not follow, it is natural to become discouraged.

Yet the hallmark of professionals is their capacity to keep priorities straight and to persevere in what their professional judgment tells them is right. It follows from this that the loyalties of professionals are toward competency, skilled judgments, and fellow professionals. Organizational attachments are secondary. Mobility is high because professionals are constantly in search of better conditions within which to practice their skills.

SELF-CRITICISM

It is difficult to be critical of oneself, or even of one's organization, but such criticism needs to be continuously applied. It takes effort, time, and difficult decisions, but it has its rewards in greater job satisfaction and in better organizational results. It identifies areas where you can work toward improvement. As examples, consider the following questions:

☐ Are your organization's advertising and public relations policies in accord with your values and expectations?

☐ Have you given specific attention to your actions and decisions that cut across the boundaries of your organization and into the boundaries of others?

☐ What mistakes have you made during the past year? What were the effects, and how could they have been avoided?

☐ Have you taken risks and responsibilities commensurate with your objectives?

☐ What important factors have you overlooked or ignored that would have enabled you to be more effective?

☐ Have you tried to learn something from every situation in which you have been involved?

Career Planning

The development of your career is so important that you should continuously devote planning effort to it. Career planning is a systematic way of anticipating and preparing future alternative opportunities in both the education and the work sectors. Your planning not only keeps you up to date with the developing demands of your current job but also with changes in the environment which affect your work. By planning you can maximize your opportunities to develop self-confidence and master the anxieties and disappointments which inevitably come with change. The need to make important choices dictates the need for planning.

Career development is evolutionary in nature. Therefore it must be related to the critical turning points in your life history. Your needs change as you grow older. One moves through stages of job preparation, first experiences, creating and raising a family, the post-family years, and retirement. Your financial needs also change as you pass through these stages. The central issue in all phases is self-understanding. Within you is a strong urge to make the most of yourself. But you are highly dependent upon organizations and upon other people for support, encouragement, and resources.

Planning is inhibited by the fact that fears and anxieties about change keep a person hanging on to the present. This may lead to overlooking impending signs of change. Career planning enables you to think ahead, to partially control the future, and to take account of emerging conditions. All too often, individuals are opportunistic in their job choices. Thus they are the victims of events rather than the master.

Also, it is easier to think about relatively short-term goals than about long-range plans. Therefore in career planning it is a good idea to think not only of short-term goals but also to consider long-range goals, a stage or two ahead of where you are at present.

A beginning step is to survey your present situation. Do you like your work? Do you like the organization you work for? Does your situation provide the satisfaction you feel it should? Further, you should review the steps by which you got the position. Your past career pattern is a clue to what your future career pattern may hold for you.

Many individuals limit their career planning to advancement to the next job in the same line of work. However, experience increasingly indicates that people in today's complex society often pursue multiple careers—that is, they change from one occupation to another. Businessmen in their early or late 50s often enter teaching as a second career, moving into it gradually through part-time teaching and finally making a permanent decision. Military or government workers often earn retirement benefits in twenty years, allowing them to make changes in their careers.

Your review of past and present experience should:

Consider your educational work history, and your accomplishments to date

Analyze the factors that have contributed to or have been associated with your career progress

Evaluate your talents in terms of your current job requirements

Organize your beliefs and concerns about the way your career
is determined and what influences it

Identify currently available resources in your work situation
for preparing and implementing your career plans

Examine the strategy you have been using either by default or
conscious choice

Synthesize the information, insights, and concerns which you
gained from the above steps

Find resource people who can help you with the above synthesis and analysis and discuss the various possibilities with
them

After you have made the above analysis, think imaginatively
about the factors which will determine your ability to function
effectively at the next stage of your career. Appraise your interests and abilities against the analysis you have made.

Implementing your career plans is an important final consideration. The steps you take will be supported by the information
you have gathered and the analysis you have made. In this step,
it is important to overcome the reluctance to change. It may be
that the changes you desire can be obtained in your present
organization. Or, you may need to change your organization or
your occupation. More education and training may be needed to
give you the credentials and abilities required in the new work.

Your career outlook should take into account the fact that our
economy has changed from being a production-centered manufacturing one into a service-oriented one. There will be a continued growth in the service sectors for the remainder of the
century. In 1971, over 60 percent of our labor force was devoted
to the production of services and only 40 percent to the production of raw materials and industrial products. This was a
watershed in our business history. By the year 2000 as much as
70 percent of our employment may be in the service industries
and only 30 percent in the production of physical goods.

Mobility

The job and geographical mobility of executives and managers is
extremely high in the United States. Mobility is an important
aspect of career development, for it enables the manager to move

more rapidly into positions of higher responsibility. Often, however, such movements present psychological problems to managers and their families for they involve serious, disruptive changes.

According to one survey, about 60 to 65 percent of all long distance moves across state lines are business-inspired. The government accounts for another 20 to 25 percent. Only in the remaining 10 to 20 percent are moves initiated by those who are moving. Another survey showed that the number of moves increased greatly in 1974. Of 282 companies surveyed, 100 said that they were increasing employee relocations, and only 39 said they were decreasing relocations. In sum, about one-fifth of the population of the United States changes addresses every year. Thus the odds for your moving within the near future are rather high.

Moving geographically either for the same company or for another organization is often a good idea for the younger or beginning executives intent upon advancement. Many new graduates of college programs find that their first job is not what they expected. Moreover, the emphasis in the early stages of one's career is on accumulating experience. Often the first job seems good when it is accepted but fails to provide the desired level of growth, satisfaction, and experience that one needs.

Many managers have firm guidelines about where they want to live. Naturally, the person who is open to any geographical location has more opportunities at his disposal. The time to avoid restrictions is when one is young and in the early stages of one's career. After marriage and acquiring a family, a manager is less flexible about making changes. Anxiety is connected with such a decision. Moving to a new community is a drastic change. New habits have to be formed. New friends have to be made. Such adjustments are particularly difficult for one's spouse and children.

Your need for stability is in conflict with your need for change. There is, first of all, an urge to maintain the status quo. Many managers remain in jobs longer than a reasonable assessment of their career objectives would indicate. On the other hand, excessive restlessness and discontent lead some to change jobs before they have developed their full potential or before they have made their fullest contribution. Excessive job-hopping tendencies have to be balanced against undue complacence.

One of the psychological problems of changing locations has to do with one's personal identity. Identity has many dimensions, including the industry in which you work, your company, your job responsibilities, your title, and your compensation. If you derive a strong sense of self-identification through your title, your responsibility, or your organization, change decisions become difficult. Once the change is made, you face the problem of affirming a new identity. On the other hand, if your present organization does not provide adequate personal identity satisfactions, you will be likely to want to seek a new job.

Vance Packard, in his book *A Nation of Strangers,** has analyzed the rootlessness that stems from high mobility. He feels that people are becoming less human, because high rates of mobility make living a succession of temporary stands. Frequent moves deprive managers and their families of a sense of community and deep, lasting friendships. While Packard strains a bit hard to make his case against mobility, he is nevertheless persuasive in relating many of society's ills, such as personal bankruptcies, soaring crime rates, the confused economy, the breakdown of the family and the rise in divorce rates and premarital and extramarital sexual relationships, at least in part to high mobility rates. People cannot be good citizens when they are indifferent to their communities and to the quality of life in them. Nomadic individuals, Packard says, tend to develop nomadic values. For people come to live only for the moment, the present is the only thing that's important.

There is evidence of a slowdown in the extent of job changes involving geographical relocation. Although millions of Americans get company transfers every year, a decline is under way because of higher costs and greater recognition of the seriousness of disruptions of family and community. Employers are encountering increasing resistance to transfers from employees concerned about the difficulties of moving, the effects on their family life, and the associated personal anxieties. According to one personnel executive, "Employers are beginning to accept the fact

*New York: David McKay Company, 1972.

that many of their most talented people don't want to become corporate gypsies. Executives are putting more value on home life, stability, and their children. Career goals no longer hold top priority, and companies have to come to grips with that."

It should be noted that mobility can benefit corporations. Some consider mobility as a kind of screening device to identify aggressive and ambitious managers. It is also a device for extracting complacent employees from the comfortable social networks they have created for themselves. It aborts parochial attitudes and breaks up overdependence on comfortable roles. Although these views are becoming less significant as employees revolt against undue transfer, there are still managers who believe that unwillingness to move for a company implies a suspicious lack of loyalty. Therefore frequent moves may serve as part of a process of initiation and testing. The man who can take it is a man on his way up, made of sterner stuff desired by higher management. Such views are more in the nature of rationalizations than reasons for high relocation rates.

Forcing a reluctant manager to move may have lasting negative effects. In one such case, a manager was forced to go on a two-year assignment to South Africa. Having just returned from extensive foreign duty, he and his family were tired of living abroad. After giving reasons for his reluctance, he acceded to the request. However, as a result of further family discussions he told his boss that he could not go. The boss then threatened him with the loss of his job, and the manager undertook the assignment. From then on the manager bore an unremitting hostility toward the boss and the company.

Mobility does help managers enlarge their experiences and acquire detailed understandings of the diversity and the special problems and characteristics of different locations. In sum, balance is needed between the forces of stability and change.

The Job Market

Since supply and demand in the job market fluctuate with economic conditions and with factors such as military conscription, educational trends, population changes, and technological change, it is important to incorporate job market information into your career planning.

Conflicting reports of job market conditions need to be assessed. Part of the discrepancy is due to the differences between long- and short-range forecasting. At any given time, the market is caught up in its tendency to fluctuate. In the short run, jobs may be scarce. For talented or specialized managers, the situation may be better than for others. Career planning envisions a long-run view. Organizations continuously need administrators and managers with insight, ability, experience, and creative talents, whatever the condition of the market. In the long-run outlook, you have less to fear if you have a record of success.

When the economy is tight and jobs are scarce, a manager does not have to be incompetent, but merely average, to be in danger of losing his job. Thinning the ranks, especially in middle management, becomes the order of the day, and the situation seems grim to anyone planning a career change or who is out of work. The best insurance against this situation is to find ways of not being ordinary. You have to be more than merely competent; you have to be good. During hard times, companies "trade up"; this is a fact of life.

In tough times, the hardest hit are managers in their 30s, especially those under 35, and those over 50 who have not made it to a senior position. Companies can often leave vacant indefinitely jobs in the $25,000 to $50,000 per year salary brackets. Also, companies may fire executives, retire them early, or slow down their advancement, not because they are incompetent, but merely because they may lack the special attributes demanded by the times.

In the long-run view, a case can be substantiated for an impending shortage of high-talent management manpower. To blame for such a shortage are the low birth rates of the 1930s, the unprecedented expansion in the size of the average corporation, the increasing complexity of managerial processes, the growing demand for executive talent by nonbusiness and nonindustrial organizations such as government and education, and the changes in the attitudes and motivations of college students that first became apparent in the 1960s.

Most corporate managers are drawn from the 35-55 age group

which was 43 percent of the labor force in 1960 but will be only 35 percent by 1980. If the motivation to manage develops in the rapidly expanding 24-34 age group, this younger group could fill the gap. Unfortunately, the motivation to manage among college students who might provide future managerial talent is low and it is falling.* The decline in motivation to manage among the younger generation reflects a tendency to reject the authority role in organizations. Many writers have pointed out the skepticism of American youth toward authority. Young people question the legitimacy and the values of established systems of authority, particularly in business and government. This attitude complicates the training and education programs that provide our nation's managers.

In the late 1970s there is evidence that values and beliefs among the young are swinging back to a more balanced perspective. In any case, the creative manager prepares for career change by observing the job market trends that are most significant. In the long-run view, the capable manager will find that challenging work is available.

Out of Work

Some time in your career, you may face the loss of your job. Tough as this is, you can turn the situation into an opportunity. Your own frame of mind is important. It is a time for a review of your aims and potentials, and a critical turning point that can pay dividends if you do some careful planning. It is a time of stress and tension for you and your family.

One's job provides, in addition to income, a center of meaning and interest. It provides social contacts, daily interactions, the meeting of challenges. It contributes to your sense of identity. Your life has been structured around a particular job in a particular setting and for particular purposes. You are now cut off from these social and psychological relationships. This, naturally, produces feelings of stress, tension, or even hostility.

Since a job is a source of personal identity and stability, unem-

*John B. Miner, *The Human Constraint: The Coming Shortage of Managerial Talent* (Washington, D.C.: BNA Books, 1974).

ployment is hard to accept. The loss of one's job can, therefore, be as debilitating psychologically as it is financially. The threat to one's psychological well-being should be squarely faced. But try not to let it detract from your energy and capability for job search.

The reason for the loss of your job has little to do with your reaction. If you already have a basically healthy self-image, you will adapt more easily and be less likely to view the job loss as a personal defeat than if you had been highly dependent or over-sensitive, seeking perfection in yourself and those around you. Keeping busy in a purposeful way is a healthy response. Idle time leads to brooding and depression. You may be helped by viewing your newly acquired spare time as an asset rather than a liability. You can get odd jobs out of the way, catch up on read-ing, or even hate your former employer, if it will help. But the best remedy is the activity and the element of success entailed in working on your career plans and getting a new job.

An estimated 500,000 managers are fired each year in the United States and suddenly confronted with the need to find a new job. It takes practice to resign or to get fired properly. In many cases it is not necessarily a disgrace. When a discharge occurs or a layoff notice arrives, remain calm, don't panic, don't explode. A dismissed manager who unleashes his anger can blemish a good record. You should first negotiate with your or-ganization for the best separation deal you can get. Find out about references and severance pay. Try to get the use of office space and a secretary while relocating. Determine whether or not such help will be charged against your severance pay.

No matter what the reason for your separation, the relation-ship between you and the organization is over. No amount of regret, sympathy or company apologies will be of practical use. The person who discharged you may feel guilty and uneasy no matter how good a front he is putting on. A gracious departure will leave a lasting impression. There is no use in spouting off to the boss. Recriminations, faultfinding, and complaining to your fellow employees are fruitless. Nothing will change, so don't create enemies. You can get people to help you, and you will need them.

If you are over 40 and can prove that you have been discharged to make room for a younger person, you have a case for reinstatement in your old job with back pay. Even if you are unwilling to file a formal case, you may at least have some ammunition with which to get better severance arrangements, such as better-than-ordinary references, more clerical help, or extra severance pay.

You don't have to live in constant fear of losing your job, but you shouldn't let it sneak up on you. Most managers who get fired could have anticipated it by paying attention to quality of their own performance or to changes in their company. Most managers are somewhat aware of their own failures and inadequacies but continue to plug away at their work without change. The more successful a person is, the less foresight he is likely to have about his performance. One generally keeps busy and doesn't take the time to think that anything could happen to him. If you sense that you're not doing well, you may want to make plans for relocating. Even though you can conduct some of your relocation plans while still on a job, it is sometimes wise to quit and devote full time to your relocation effort. In any case, it is not smart to keep turning in poor performances.

You can look for some danger signals that may indicate a cutback in personnel in your organization. For example, your industry may be declining, technology changing, or new practices developing. Your company may be slipping relative to others in its industry. Among the questions you should ask are: How long have I been on my present job? Has my boss conveyed any dissatisfaction with my work? Am I vulnerable to a possible reorganization? When such signals are noticed it is time to freshen up your resume. Regardless of how solid your current job seems or how comfortable you feel, always keep in mind what your next career step might be, particularly if some unforeseen event occurs.

When this change looms, allow or persuade the company to fire you properly. Try to define a "no-fault" reason for being fired. If you can do this with honesty, you will have created your own references. For example, a change in organization may explain why there is no place left for you. It is better to face your discharge openly with your neighbors, friends, and others who may help you. While it may be tempting to act as though nothing has happened, an important event has occurred. What you need is a direct attack on your problem. In activity you will find the possibility for restoring and rebuilding your confidence. The dismissal may be a crisis that will represent a turning point in your career.

Job Finding

Once out of work, it is a good idea to make a clean break from the old situation. There is no need to "clean things up at the office," to finish projects or to organize things for your successor. Usually time spent resting, vacationing, lunching with friends and former associates, pretending to be a consultant, or daydreaming about going into business for yourself is a waste of time. The thing to do is to start serious job hunting from the first hour of your separation.

Map an overall strategy which includes a budget analysis for your financial situation, a timetable of activities, and specific goals. You will also want to include some target job opportunities, together with library research on the organizations you pick for initial exploration. Review your resume to make sure it is up to date and in the best possible form. Your objective then becomes one of getting interviews, preparing for interviews, and following up on the interviews you obtain. A review of your career plans will indicate whether it is time to change fields, what kind of position you are going to seek, whether or not you will take a pay cut, and whether you will relocate.

It will cost money for you to conduct a job search. Your budget should include a minimum of $200 a month for job hunting costs, exclusive of fees for counseling or psychological tests. It is not a good idea to cut corners that result in poor appearance or cheap-looking resumes. The principal cost factors may include travel to conventions (where you can see a large number of potential employers), revising and printing resumes, telephone charges, and postage and other mailing costs. The potential of mass mailings should not be overlooked. One executive mailed out 5,000 letters in the effort to relocate.

Writing a letter of application and developing a resume is an art form which you may not have had the opportunity to practice very often. In preparing the resume, you have to decide what goes in, what should be left out, what format you should use, what tone and impression you want to create, and what kind of letter goes with it. The resume should be kept short. You should probably aim for two or not more than three pages. Your work history should be complete but concentrate on the most recent jobs. Windy, idealistic statements of career jobs, broad philosophies, and puffery about what you can do for your new employer are wasted space. Avoid vague, general statements; the more specific you can be, the better. Also, it is important that the resume be an honest one. Catching you in a lie, a distortion, or an undue exaggeration can turn a prospective employer off fast, and there are ways of checking what you have said.

You have to steer a steady course between telling people enough and telling them too much. You don't want to discourage the reader from feeling that he can learn more about you from an interview nor do you want to overwhelm him with too much detail. You may have to make successive drafts of your resume, testing it out in some dry-run situations to bring it up to the proper quality.

The most difficult part of job hunting is getting an interview. Your intervention into the organization of a possible employer is complicated by the fact that the people you need to see are going to be the busiest. You will not be able to get interviews in all of your selected companies. However, if you write a good letter of application, enclose a brief version of your resume, and request a personal appointment, you will have the best chance of getting several interviews among your target company group.

How to conduct yourself once an interview is obtained is another problem. You should appear at the interview already knowing a lot about the organization you are visiting. Make your genuine interest clear. By examining annual reports and other information about the company, you will have a strong base to work from. In most cases, it is good to take a fairly aggressive role in the initial interviews. Think about what the interviewer is basically looking for: someone who can make money for his company or make his job easier, perhaps. He is probably not a professional interviewer, and he may refer you to the personnel department where professional interviewers can take you apart. The object of the interview is to get an offer. You should probably behave in such a way as to get a serious offer even if it becomes apparent you may not want the job. If you have offers already, that fact will improve your strength in getting other interviews.

Dealing with Headhunters and Job Counselors

When the demand for middle and senior executives is running high, the activities of corporate headhunters increase. The headhunter is a search consultant who contracts with organizations to find key and often specialized job candidates. You need a strategy for dealing with them. The first thing to do when you are contacted by such a recruiter is to tell him you will call back. You can then check the reliability of his firm with those who have used it or with other knowledgeable people. While most such firms are legitimate, there are "fast operators" who are trying to get big fees by playing a game called musical chairs.

If the search consultant wants you to pay a fee, it is fairly certain that he is not operating properly. Reputable recruiting firms get paid by the hiring organization, not by the individuals they place. Also, if the recruiter does not identify his client and inform you completely about him, you probably will not want to continue the discussions.

One good strategy is to ask a lot of questions and to evaluate the information. A good recruiter will not try to talk you into taking a job that is too risky or one for which you are not properly qualified. If you take the job under such circumstances and become unhappy, you lose, and the reputation of the recruiter suffers. Basically, his goal is to find and screen a group of qualified candidates and pick a few that he can recommend to his client.

Be frank with the recruiter. Any information you give him can be easily checked so it doesn't pay to alter the truth. The recruiter can help you to get a better picture of yourself as a person, with a fair assessment of your strengths and weaknesses. You can also use him as a sounding board or a bumper in your negotiations if things progress. The recruiter can suggest ways that will help your negotiations jell.

When you are faced with the necessity of immediate job relocation, you may be able to develop and carry out strategies entirely on your own. However, job counseling services are available, and you may decide to find one to help you. Job counselors are very similar to headhunters in that they know market situations and job availabilities and have the basis for assessing job candidates. If they render a large amount of personalized service such as helping to design resumes, testing, and other analytical procedures, they may legitimately charge a fee. While this personalized service is not always necessary, you may find it desirable. However, this field is full of quacks and frauds who are after high fees and do not give you much for your money. You should check on their qualifications very carefully before entering into agreements with them.

Conclusions

If you are a manager now, you have elected to play the organization game. If you perceive that your advancing career can best be followed as a member of an organization, your objective is to understand how the organization of which you are a part functions. You have to study it to determine how it affects you and how you can influence it.

You need the organization and it needs you, although the needs are not necessarily equal. The ways in which an organization activates its demands upon you and in which you pursue the needs it fulfills for you constitute the game of management. This is not a mere analogy. The management game is a hard, inevitable reality of modern life for many people today.

Games are complex mixtures of goals, risks, strategies, skills, efforts, and rewards. They have definitive rules of conduct to guide the competitive actions against opponents, although they are meant to be fun. In simple games played primarily for fun, such as gin rummy, these game elements are relatively clear and are known by all those playing the game. But in the complex games played in organizations, ground rules are hazy and unstable, and rules are applied differentially. Goals are always changing, and the risks often unclear. Strategies and skills are not always predictable or reliable. And for many, the fun easily fades or is never experienced.

Yet an organization is a tool or a device for achieving human

ends not otherwise possible. It is an imperfect tool, full of pitfalls
and disappointment for the unwary. The alternatives are either
to try for success within the limits of organizational life or to enter
occupations not closely tied to organizations. One can be a door-
to-door salesman, a newsstand operator, or a consultant or other
professional in solo practice. One can become an entrepreneur
and try to build his own organization the way he wants it. But
these options, too, have their constraints and disadvantages. For
the most part, and for most people, being an employee of a
complex organization is the best alternative.

There are those who decry or ignore the elements of gamesmanship as an interpretation of behavior in organizations. "It is
too serious a matter to call it a game," they may say. This much is
true: the elements of fun, optimism, and challenge are often hard
to come by. But in every organization, the factors of personal
goals, strategies, power, influence, and achievement are always
present, whether acknowledged or not.

The theme of creative managerial action has been employed in
this book precisely to inform the reader more fully about aspects
of the management game that are subject to his influence and
that play a part in managerial success. The concept of creative
managerial action is an optimistic one. It reveals that alternative
strategies for successful performance are more numerous than
many managers realize. Creative managerial action rests upon
the twin concepts of self-understanding and organizational
analysis. Moving on these two fronts fosters self-confidence and
faith that success, if earned, will materialize.

To speak of management and organizational life as a game is
taken by many to mean a power struggle with self-
aggrandizement and power as the ultimate prize. This is a distortion more appropriate for power-centered, self-oriented managers than ultimate winners in the game. Power may be desired
for a number of reasons: it gives one a greater piece of the pie; it
enhances egos; it drives an organization forward; it makes certain
accomplishments possible; it is a reality of life. But power also
contains its inner tensions and constraints: its disappointments
and failures are dramatized; it produces countervailing forces; it
is tied to situations that change; its permanance and benefits are
often illusory. Therefore, to blindly pursue power for power's

sake or selfish purpose is to set up the conditions for ultimate defeat. On the other hand, the wise and judicious use of power for the benefit of man, organization, and society is a legitimate, though not the sole, part of the game.

Suggested Readings

This is a list of selected references for those who wish to explore the ideas analyzed in this book. The emphasis is on source materials that reflect practical, creative strategies for managerial action.

Management and Managers

Cleveland, Harlan, *The Future Executive*. New York: Harper & Row, 1972.

Drucker, Peter F., *The Effective Executive*. New York: Harper & Row, 1967.

Duncan, W. Jack, *Decision Making and Social Issues*. Hinsdale, Ill.: The Dryden Press, 1973.

Ewing, David, *The Human Side of Planning*. New York: Macmillan, 1968.

Golde, Robert A., *Muddling Through: The Art of Properly Unbusinesslike Management*. AMACOM, 1976.

Jay, Antony, *Management and Machiavelli*. New York: Holt, Rinehart, & Winston, 1967.

McMurry, Robert N., *The Maverick Executive*. AMACOM, 1974.

Miner, John B., *The Human Constraint: The Coming Shortage of Managerial Talent*. Washington, D.C.: BNA Books, Inc., 1974.

Mintzberg, Henry, *The Nature of Managerial Work*. New York: Harper & Row, 1973.

Reeves, Elton T., *Practicing Effective Management*. AMACOM, 1975.

Rothschild, William E., *Putting It All Together*. AMACOM, 1976.

Sayles, Leonard, *Managerial Behavior: Administration in Complex Organizations*. New York: McGraw-Hill Book Company, 1971.

Sayles, Leonard, and Dowling, William F., *How Managers Motivate: The Imperatives of Supervision*. New York: McGraw-Hill Book Company, 1971.

Vance, Charles C., *Manager Today, Executive Tomorrow*. New York: McGraw-Hill Book Company, 1974.

Creativity and Problem Solving

Bach, George R., and Goldberg, Herb, *Creative Aggression*. Garden City, N.Y.: Doubleday & Company, 1974.

Buskirk, Richard H., *Handbook of Managerial Tactics*. Boston: Cahners Publishing Co., Inc., 1976.

Byrd, Richard E., *A Guide to Personal Risk Taking*. AMACOM, 1974.

188   Action Strategies for Managerial Achievement

deBono, Edward, *Lateral Thinking: Creativity Step by Step*. New York: Harper & Row, 1970.
Kobayashi, Shigeru, *Creative Management*. AMACOM, 1971.
Low, Albert, *Zen and Creative Management*. Garden City, N.Y.: Anchor Press/Doubleday, 1976.
May, Rollo, *The Courage to Create*. New York: W. W. Norton & Company, 1975.
Osborne, Alex F., *Applied Imagination*. New York: Charles Scribner's Sons, 1963.
Rickards, T., *Problem-Solving Through Creative Analysis*. New York: John Wiley & Sons, 1974.
Schleh, Edward C., *The Management Tactician*. New York: McGraw-Hill Book Company, 1974.

Organizational Analysis

Albano, Charles (ed.), *Transactional Analysis on the Job and Communicating with Subordinates*. AMACOM, 1976.
Culbert, Samuel A., *The Organization Trap: And How to Get Out of It*. New York: Basic Books, Inc., 1974.
Jay, Antony, *Corporation Man*. New York: Random House, 1971.
Koehler, Jerry, *The Corporation Game: How to Win the War with the Organization and Make Them Love It*. New York: Macmillan, 1975.
Rosenberg, Seymour, *Self-Analysis of Your Organization*. AMACOM, 1974.
Vance, Charles C., *Boss Psychology*. New York: McGraw-Hill Book Company, 1975.

Personal Development

Bliss, Edwin C., *Getting Things Done: The ABC's of Time Management*. AMACOM, 1976.
Golder, Dan, and Leggs, Karen, *Managerial Stress*. New York: John Wiley & Sons, 1975.
Kaufman, Harold G., *Obsolescence and Professional Career Development*. AMACOM, 1974.
Maas, Henry, and Kuypers, Joseph, *From Thirty to Seventy*. San Francisco: Jossey-Bass Publishers, 1975.
Mackenzie, R. Alec, *The Time Trap*. AMACOM, 1972.
Pearse, Robert F., and Pelzer, B. Purdy, *Self-Directed Change for the Mid-Career Manager*. AMACOM, 1975.
McLean, Preston, and Jillson, Katherine, *The Manager and Self-Respect*. AMACOM, 1975.
Steinchohn, Peter J., *Questions and Answers About Nerves, Tension, and Fatigue*. New York: Hawthorne Books, Inc., 1974.

Tarrant, John J., *How to Negotiate an Increase in Salary.* New York: Van Nostrand Reinhold, 1976.

Tournier, Paul, *Learn to Grow Old.* New York: Harper & Row, 1972.

Jobs and Careers

Biggs, Don, *Breaking Out of a Job You Don't Like.* New York: David McKay Company, 1973.

Blackledge, Walter, Blackledge, Ethel, and Keily, Helen, *The Job You Want–How to Get It.* Cincinnati: South-Western Publishing Company, 1975.

Haldane, Bernard, *Career Satisfaction and Success: A Guide to Job Freedom.* AMACOM, 1974.

Howell, Barbara, *Don't Bother to Come in Monday: What to Do When You Lose Your Job.* New York: St. Martin's Press, Inc., 1973.

The Job Hunting Guide. Boston: Herman Publishing Company, 1975.

Kaufman, Harold G. (ed.), *Career Management: A Guide to Combatting Obsolescence.* New York: IEEE Press, 1975.

Taylor, Phoebe, *How to Succeed in the Business of Finding a Job.* New York: Nelson Hall, Inc., 1975.

Uris, Auren, and Tarrant, Jack, *How to Keep From Getting Fired.* Chicago: Henry Regnery Co., 1975.

Women and Wives

Burger, Ninki Hart, *The Executive's Wife.* New York: Macmillan, 1968.

Dienstag, Eleanor, *Whither Thou Goest.* New York: E. P. Dutton, 1976.

Gordon, Francine E., and Strober, Myra H. (eds.), *Bringing Women into Management.* New York: McGraw-Hill Book Company, 1975.

Higginson, Margaret V., and Quick, Thomas L., *The Ambitious Woman's Guide to a Successful Career.* AMACOM, 1975.

Lewis, Alfred Allan, and Berns, Barrie, *Three Out of Four Wives.* New York: Macmillan, 1975.

Lynch, Edith M., *The Executive Suite–Feminine Style.* AMACOM, 1973.

Rogalin, Wilma C., and Pell, Arthur R., *Woman's Guide to Management Positions.* New York: Simon & Schuster, 1975.

Seidenberg, Robert, *Corporate Wives–Corporate Casualties?* AMACOM, 1973.

Index

accomplishment
  alternating working and
    planning sessions in, 158
  change-agent role in, 120
  communication in, 112–116
  conformity and, 122–123
  consultants and, 120–122
  in leadership, 118–120
  maximum results in, 110–123
  minimum conditions for, 110
  self-knowledge and, 159–161
  time management and, 153–157
  in women's colleges, 132
active manager
  communication skills of, 14
  courage of, 12
  vs. passive, 10–12
adjudication, in team building, 84
advancement, "fast" system of, 73
affirmative action, concept of, 136
aging, effectiveness and, 165–166
American Management
    Associations, 140
Arrington, Lloyd M., 41 n.
aspiration level, power and, 36
authority, creativity and, 9–10

Bass, Bernard M., 123 n.
boss
  acceptance and rejection by,
    69–71
  confrontation with, 69
  helpful suggestions to, 72

hierarchy and, 62–65
influence of, 61
mutuality of interests with, 76
practical considerations in
    relation to, 72–75
relating to, 65–66
self-confidence and, 70–71
son of, 74
upward focus and, 66–69
working with, 61–75
bottom-up management, 93
boundaries, territorial, 47
boundary spanners, 47–49
Burns, Barrie, 146 n.
Buskirk, Richard A., 37 n.

career, unusual alternatives in, 41
career development, evolutionary
    nature of, 171–172
career mavericks, 41
career planning
  indifference to, 40
  inhibition of, 172
  job market and, 177
  job satisfaction and, 171–173
career strategy, 39–44
  mid-career crisis and, 44–45
  opsimaths and, 45
  see also strategy
  "ping-pong" type, 42
career woman
  breakthrough for, 125–126
  salaries of, 131

191